ACTIVITY BOOK

FOR KIDS

- WORD SEARCH
- DOT-TO-DOT
- COLORING
- DRAWING
- COUNTING
- MAZES

AGES 3-10

This Book Belongs to:

FOR A LITTLE INSPIRATION
follow along at:

◎   @JUNEANDLUCY

f   @JUNEANDLUCY

WWW. JUNELUCY.COM

Shop our other books at
www.junelucy.com

For questions and customer service, email us at
support@junelucy.com

Hey Parents!

Sign up for our June & Lucy Kids newsletter to receive a FREE digital download of this BONUS Kid's Activity Book!

Sign up at:

http://freebies.junelucy.com/kiddos

HOW MANY GHOSTS DO YOU SEE?

I SEE _____ GHOSTS

COMPLETE THE PICTURE

MATCH WORD TO PICTURE

LLAMA

BAT

MOON

HAT

PUMPKIN

CAKE

CANDY

CACTUS

CUPCAKE

FIND THE TEN DIFFERENCES BETWEEN THE TWO PICTURES

COUNT AND COLOR

FIND 2 MATCHING ITEMS

```
M I N J I O N
O L L A M A R
O A H G F M J
N C A N D Y Q
I G T V L Y J
P U M P K I N
B A T A X X D
```

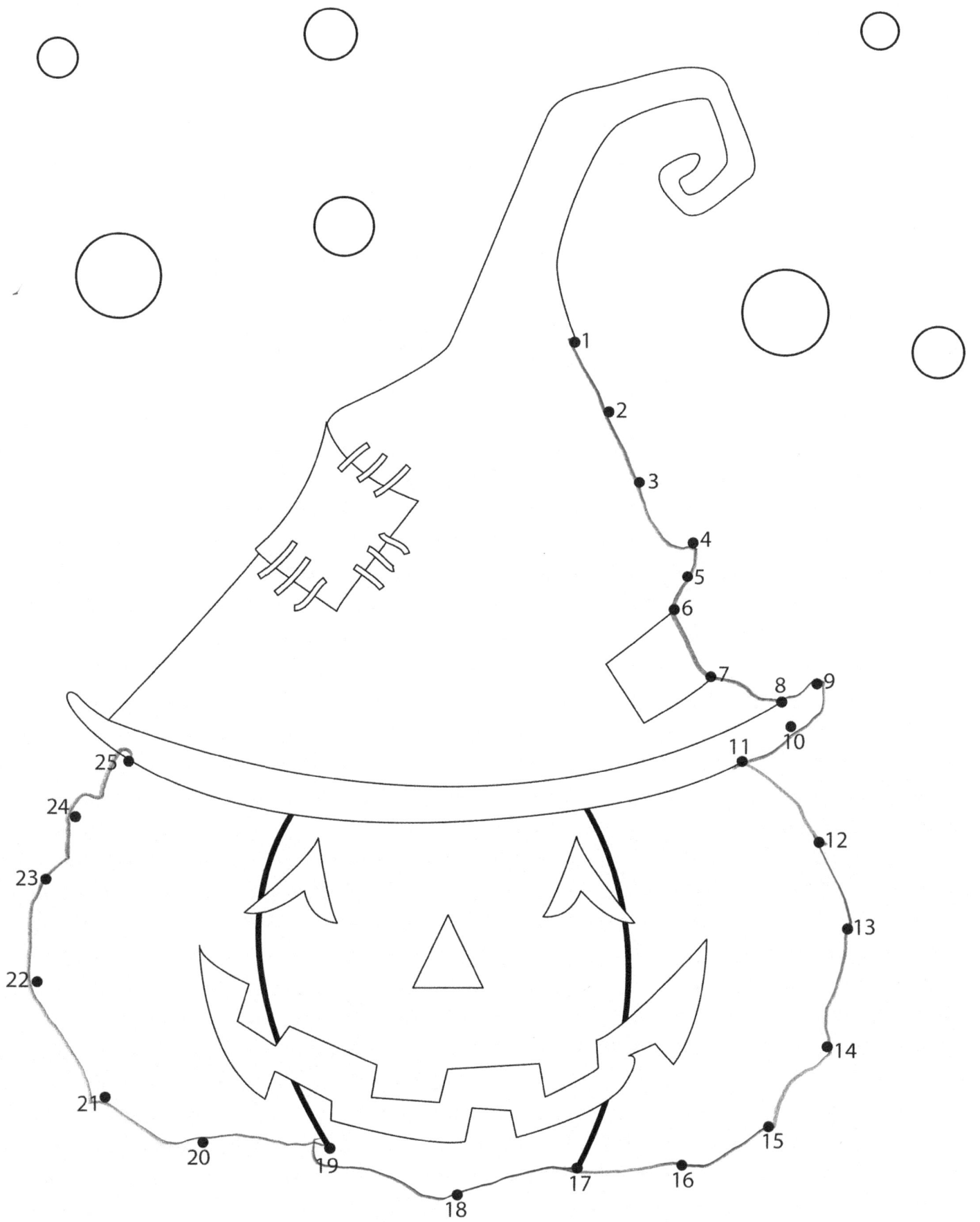

COPY THE PICTURE

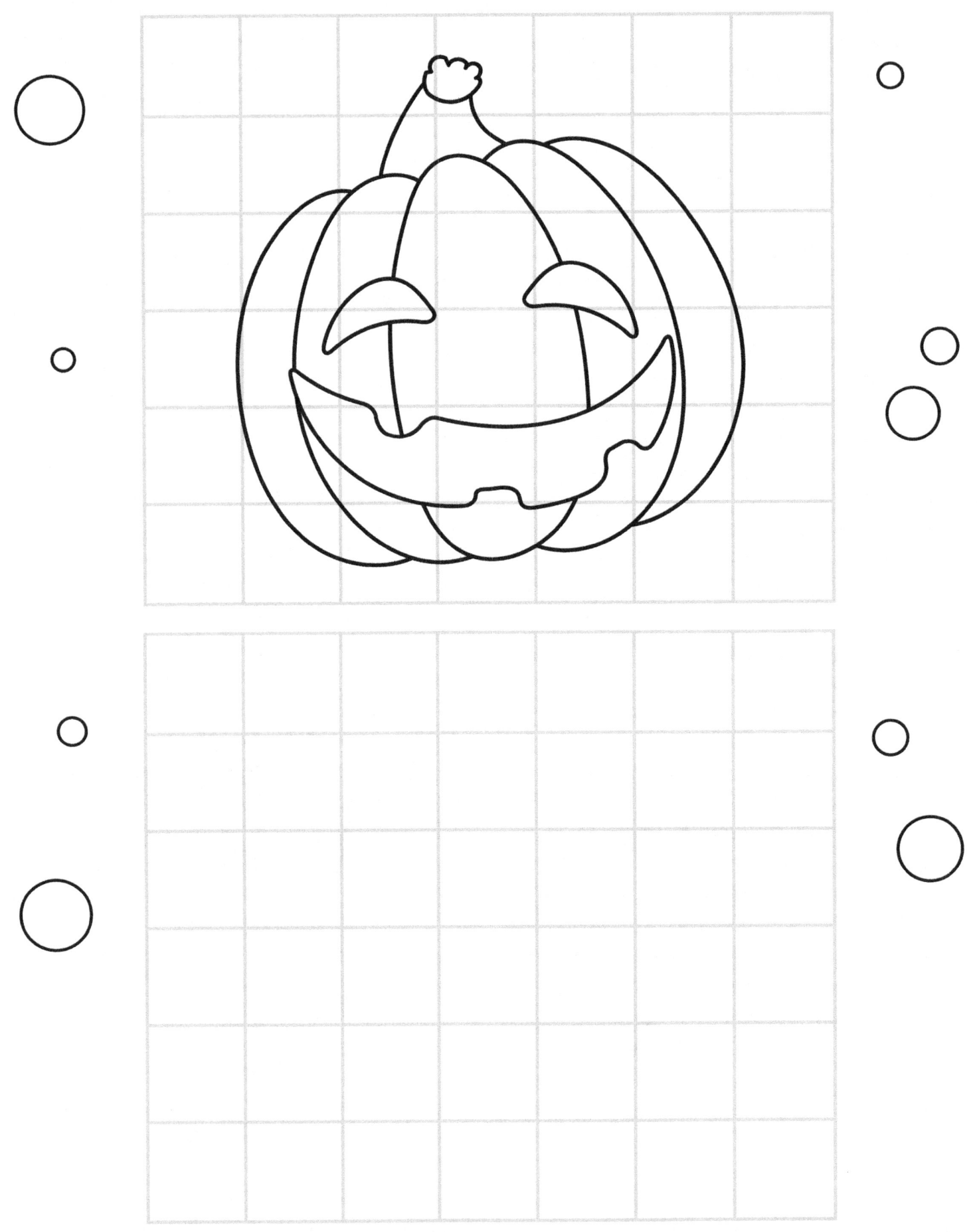

HOW MANY EGGS DO YOU SEE?

I SEE _____ EGGS

COMPLETE THE PICTURE

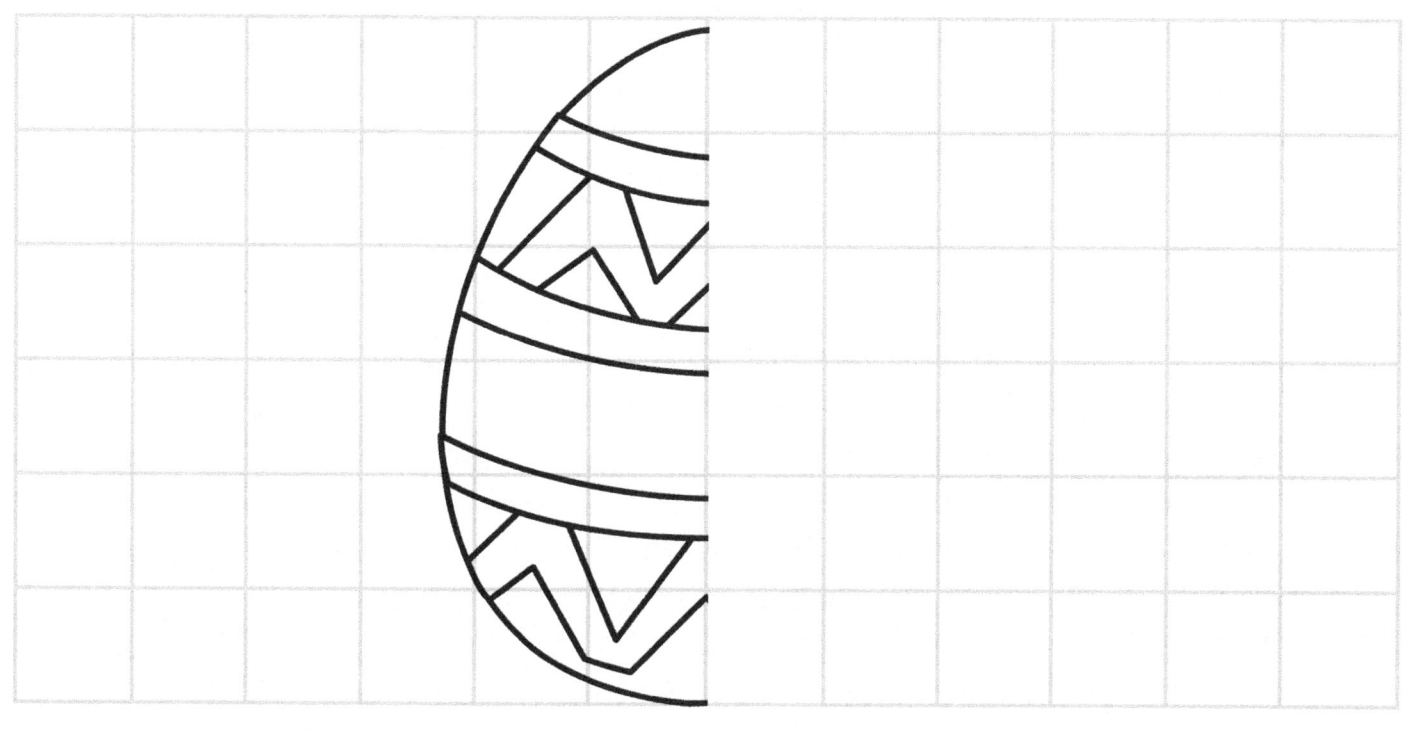

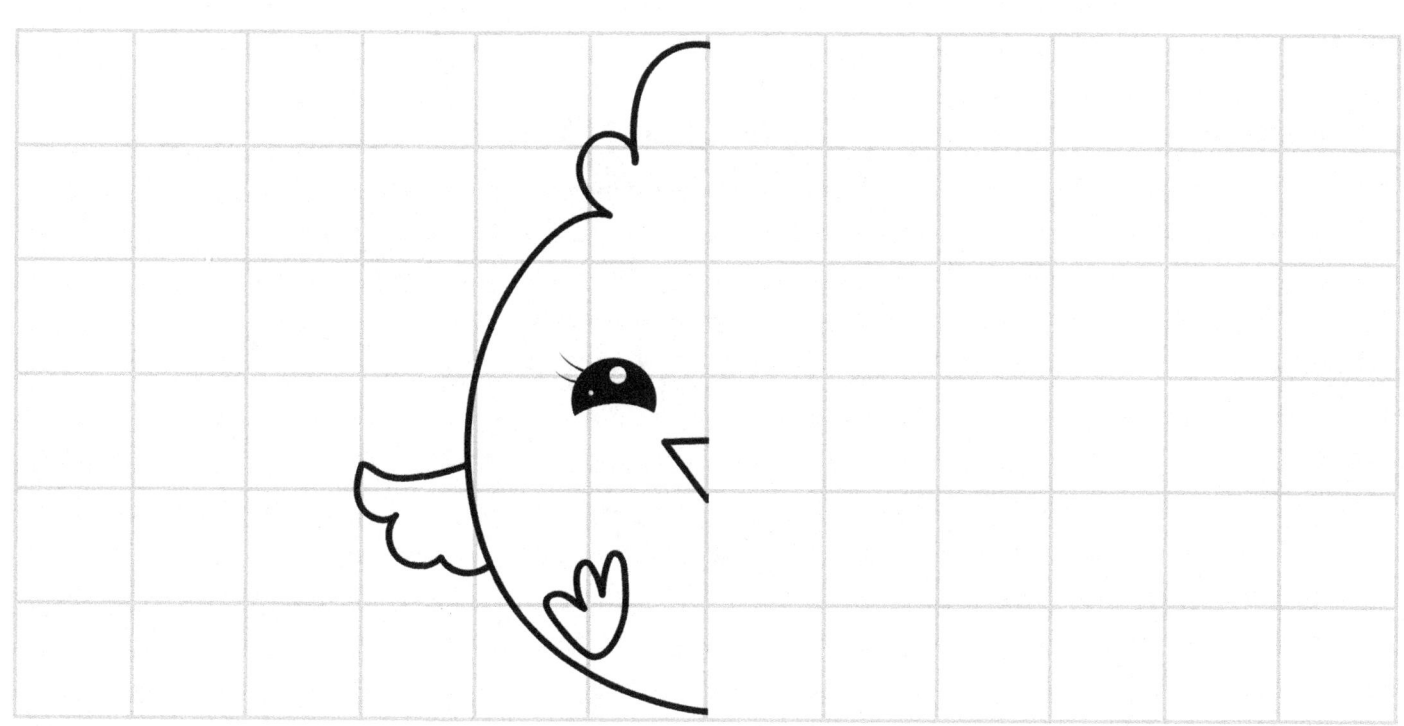

MATCH WORD TO PICTURE

BRUSH

EGGS

BASKET

CANDY

OWL

GLASSES

BUTTERFLY

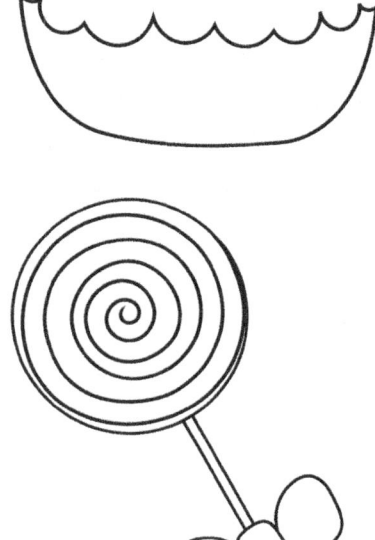

BOW

CUPCAKE

FIND THE TEN DIFFERENCES BETWEEN THE TWO PICTURES

COUNT AND COLOR

FIND 2 MATCHING ITEMS

```
T O C A R R O T T
T B A S K E T P D
O A U X E X I O
W M A O J K P N
M L L K U M Y U
C H I C K E N T
U O F L O W E R
Z O K K H M G Q
```

COPY THE PICTURE

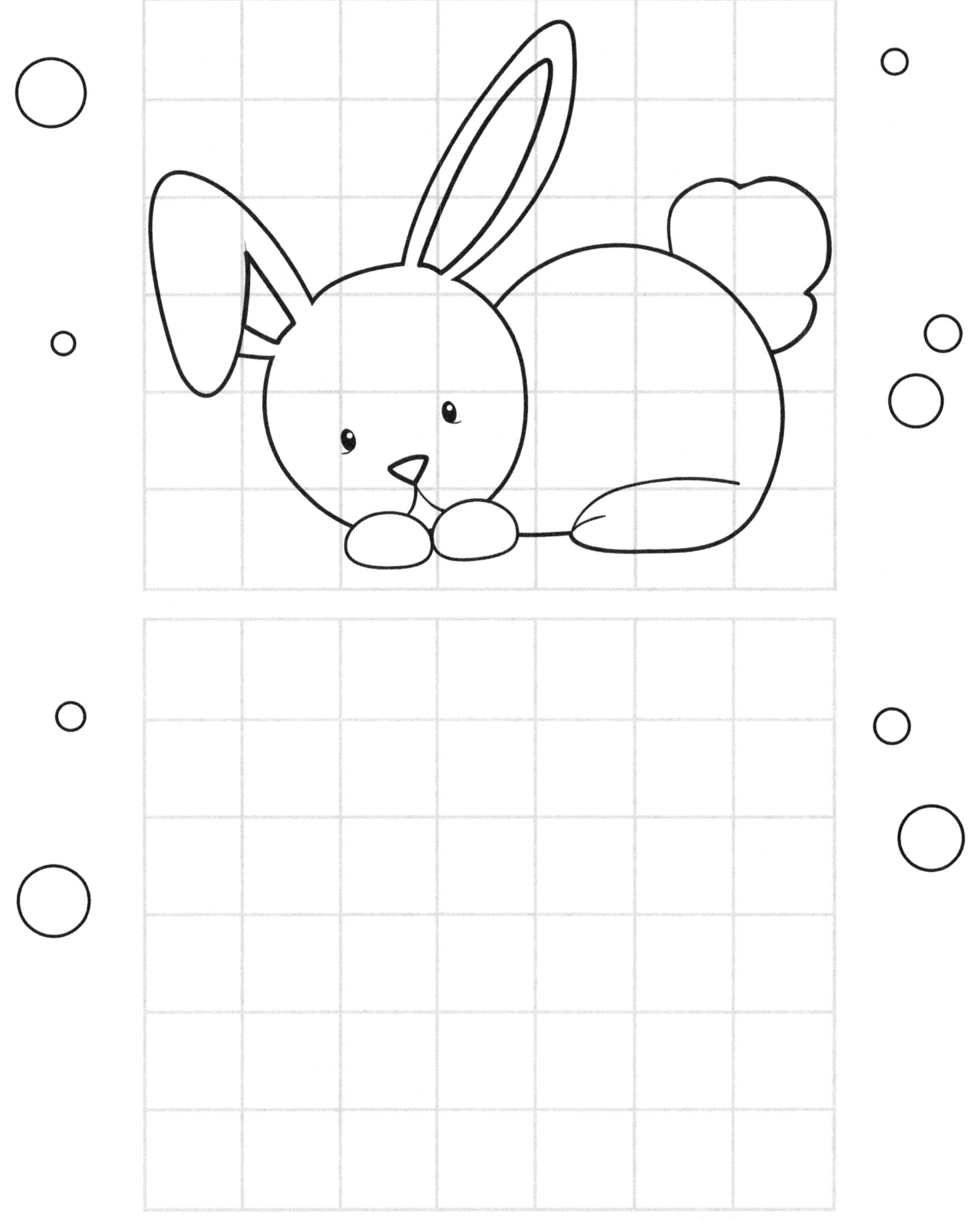

COMPLETE THE PICTURE

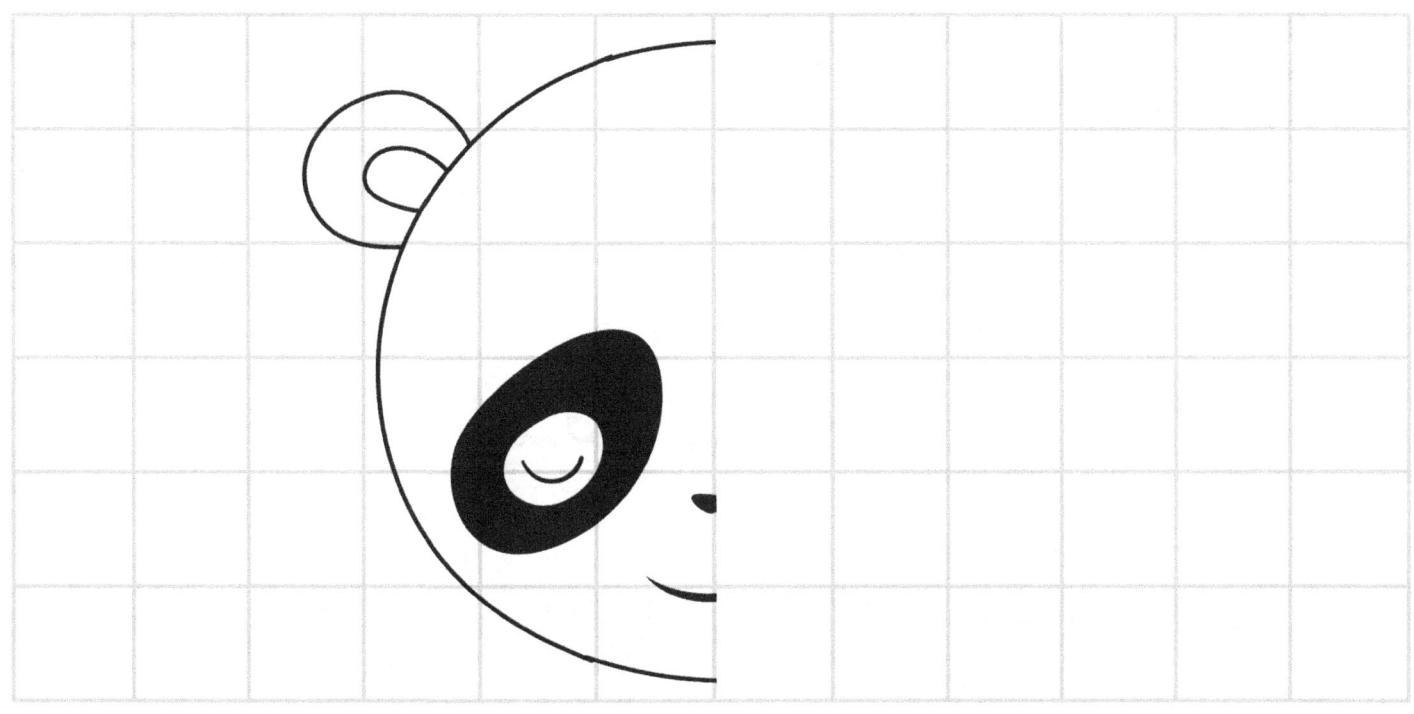

MATCH WORD TO PICTURE

FOXES

BEAR

STRAWBERRY

UNICORN

MAILBOX

WHALE

RABBIT

CHERRIES

FIND THE TEN DIFFERENCES BETWEEN THE TWO PICTURES

COUNT AND COLOR

FIND 2 MATCHING ITEMS

B	G	H	E	A	M	D	A
Q	G	I	F	T	B	T	G
C	U	N	I	C	O	R	N
B	E	A	R	W	V	V	W	C
E	L	E	P	H	A	N	T
Q	W	X	C	A	T	P	H
K	C	X	C	L	X	R	N
T	C	B	L	E	O	H	M

COPY THE PICTURE

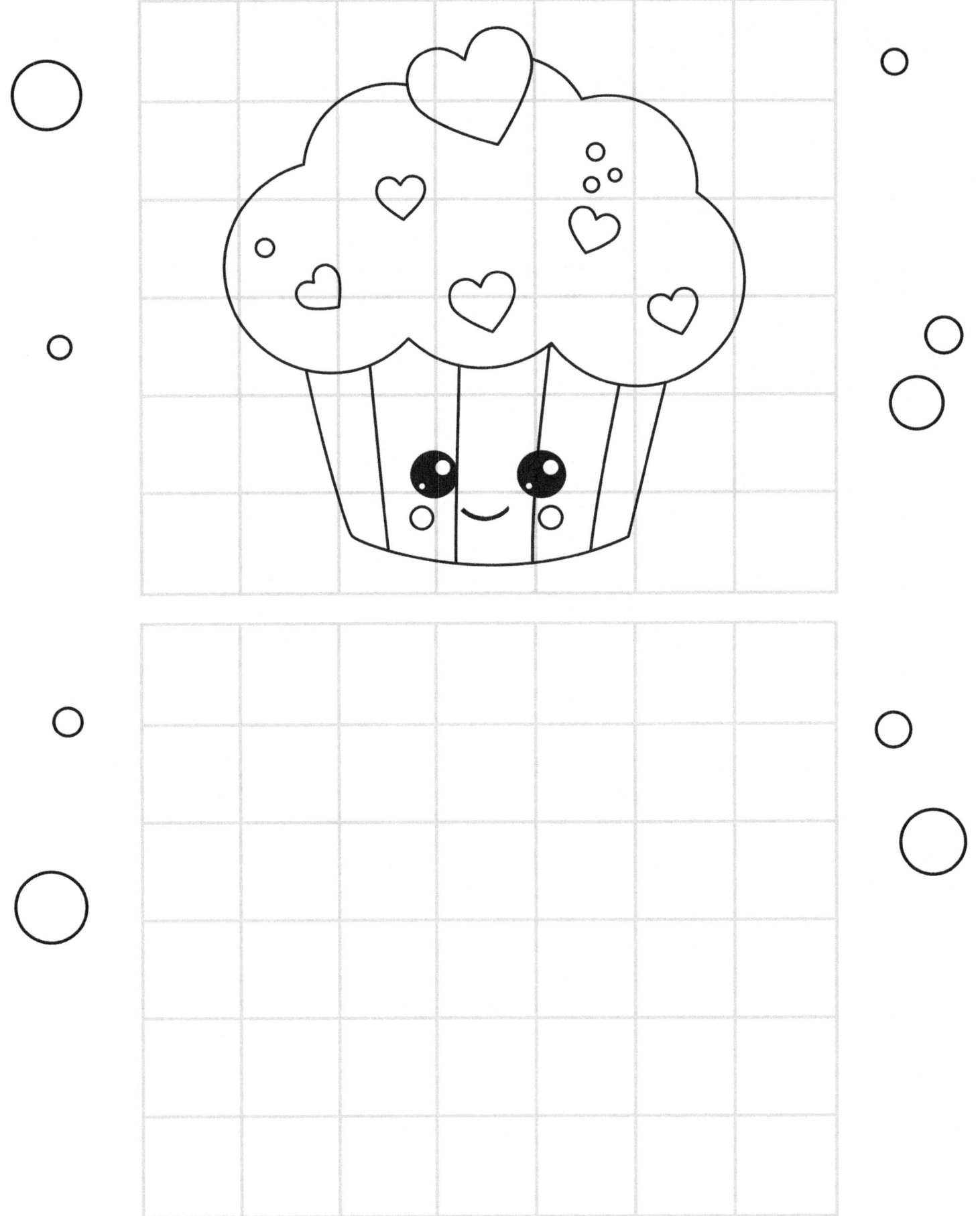

COMPLETE THE PICTURE

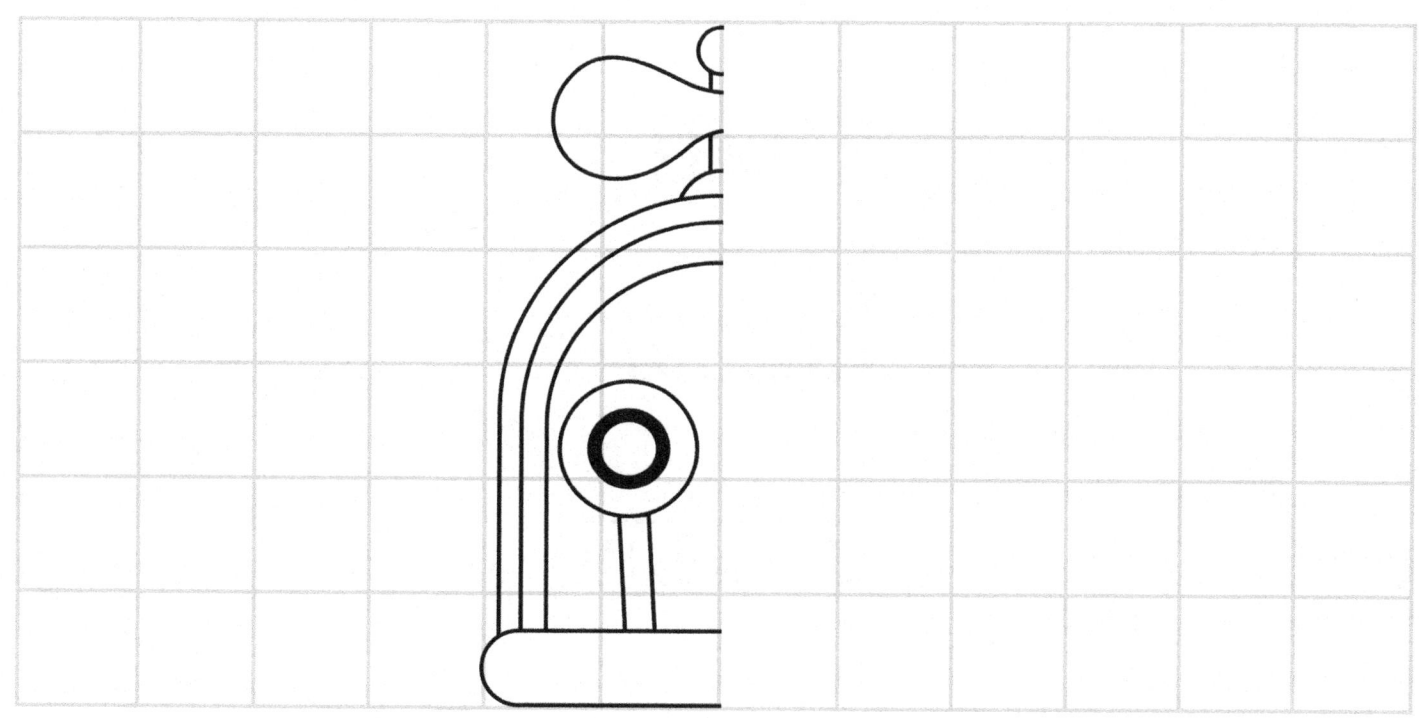

MATCH WORD TO PICTURE

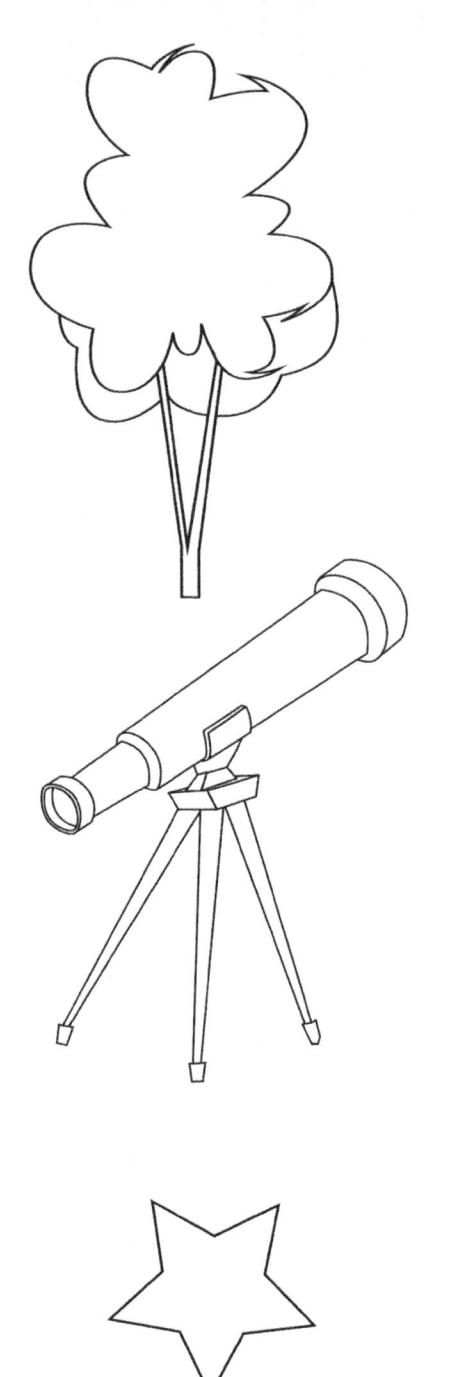

PLANET

STAR

BALL

SPYGLASS

SCREWDRIVER

TREE

ROBOT

CAMERA

KEY

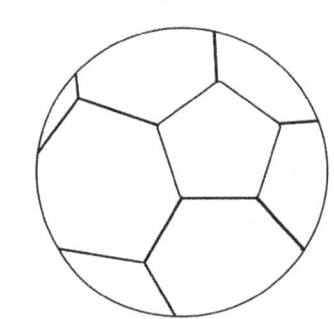

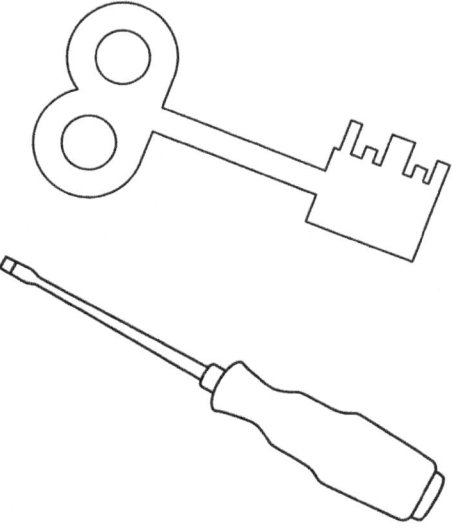

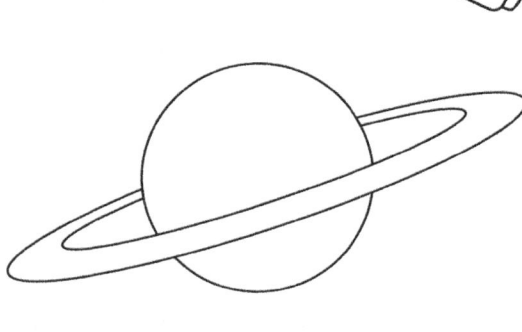

FIND THE TEN DIFFERENCES BETWEEN THE TWO PICTURES

COUNT AND COLOR

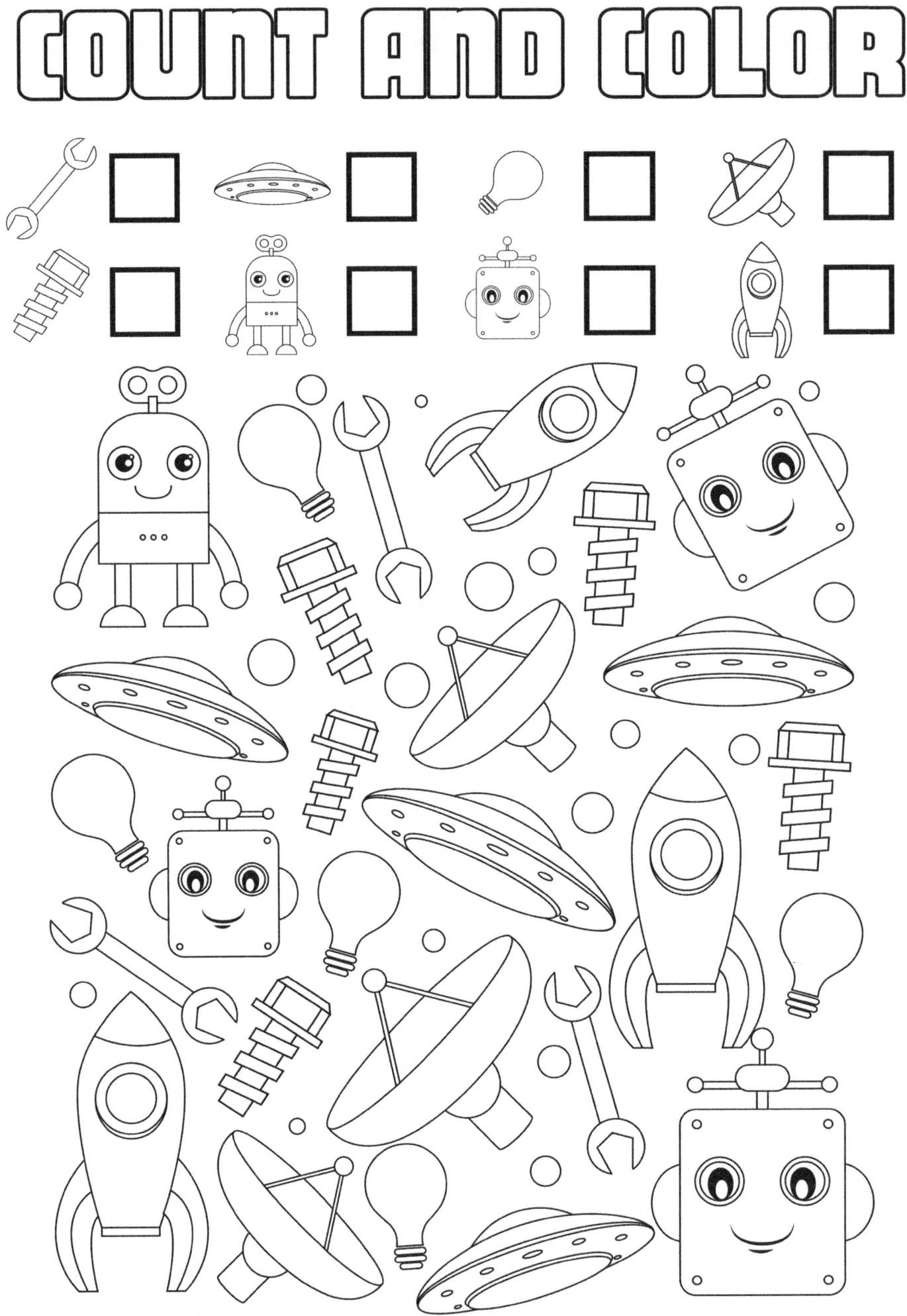

FIND 2 MATCHING ITEMS

C	I	C	A	M	E	R	A	V	S
P	S	T	S	Z	A	J	E	D	K
L	F	T	J	M	G	E	W	R	A
A	K	C	T	K	N	M	Q	O	T
N	S	F	B	G	C	O	C	B	E
E	H	U	A	O	C	M	P	O	B
T	C	A	L	F	A	Z	U	T	O
J	T	T	L	N	T	R	E	E	A
B	P	X	H	K	H	D	B	U	R
P	G	C	Z	P	Z	M	A	O	D

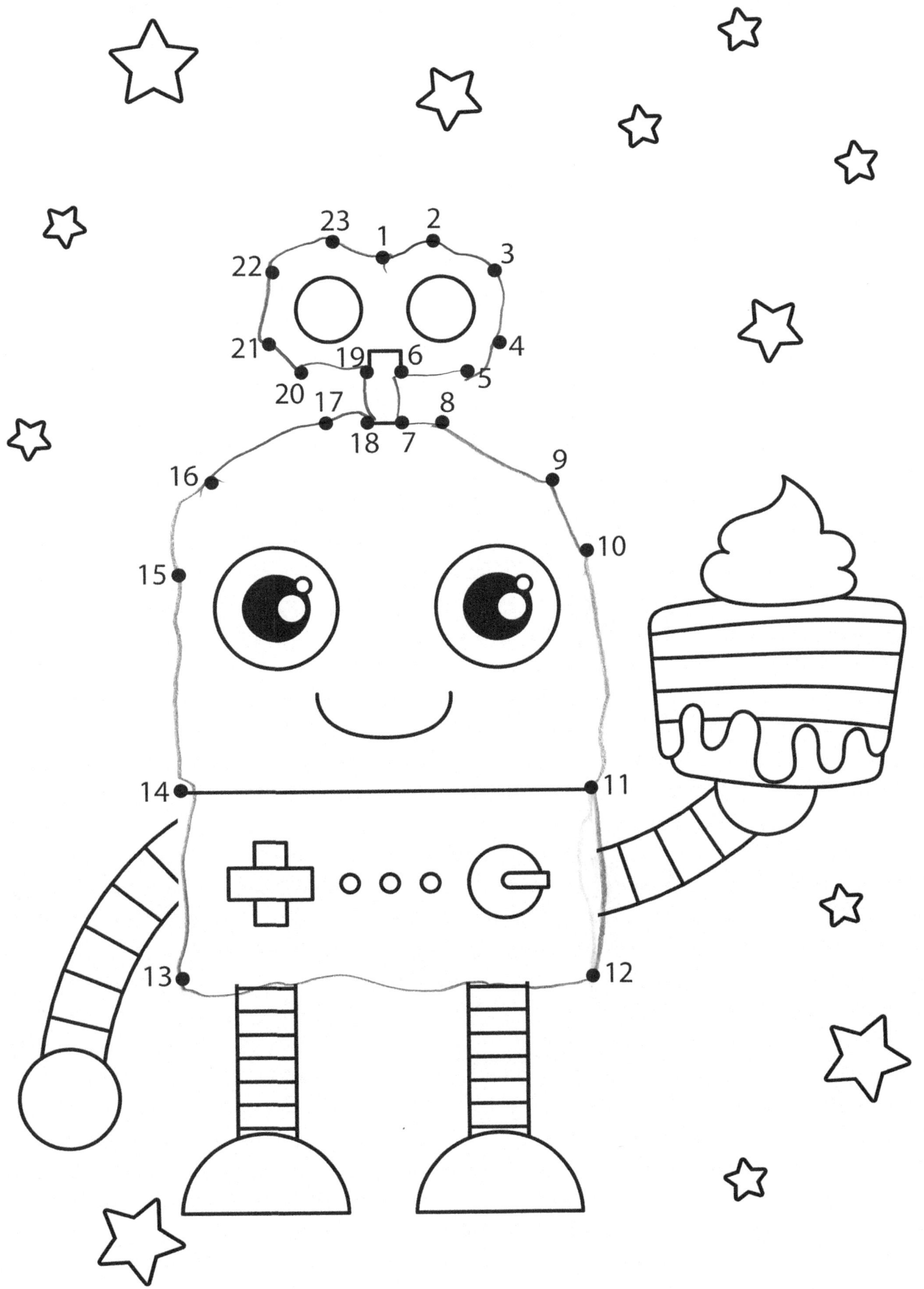

COPY THE PICTURE

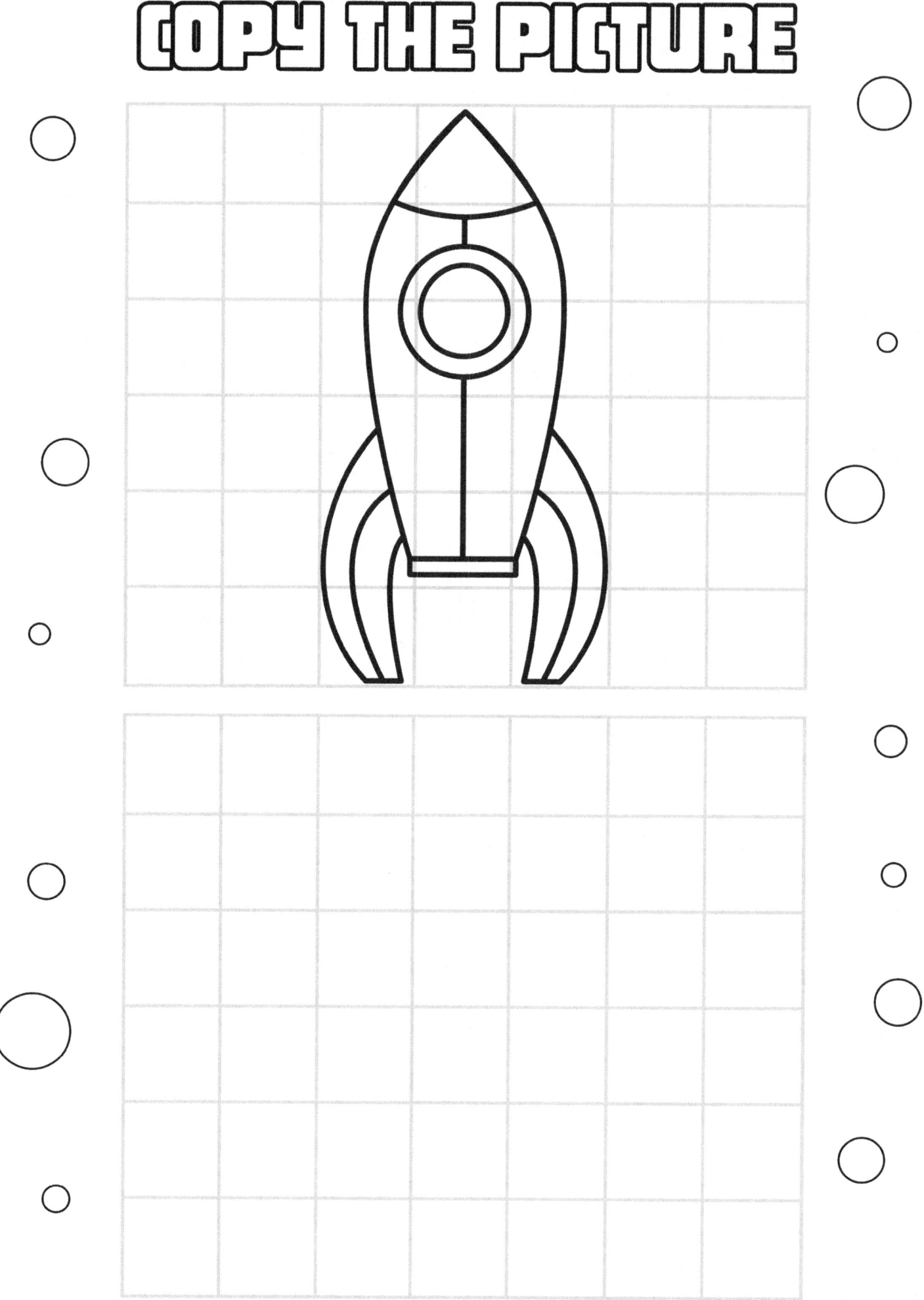

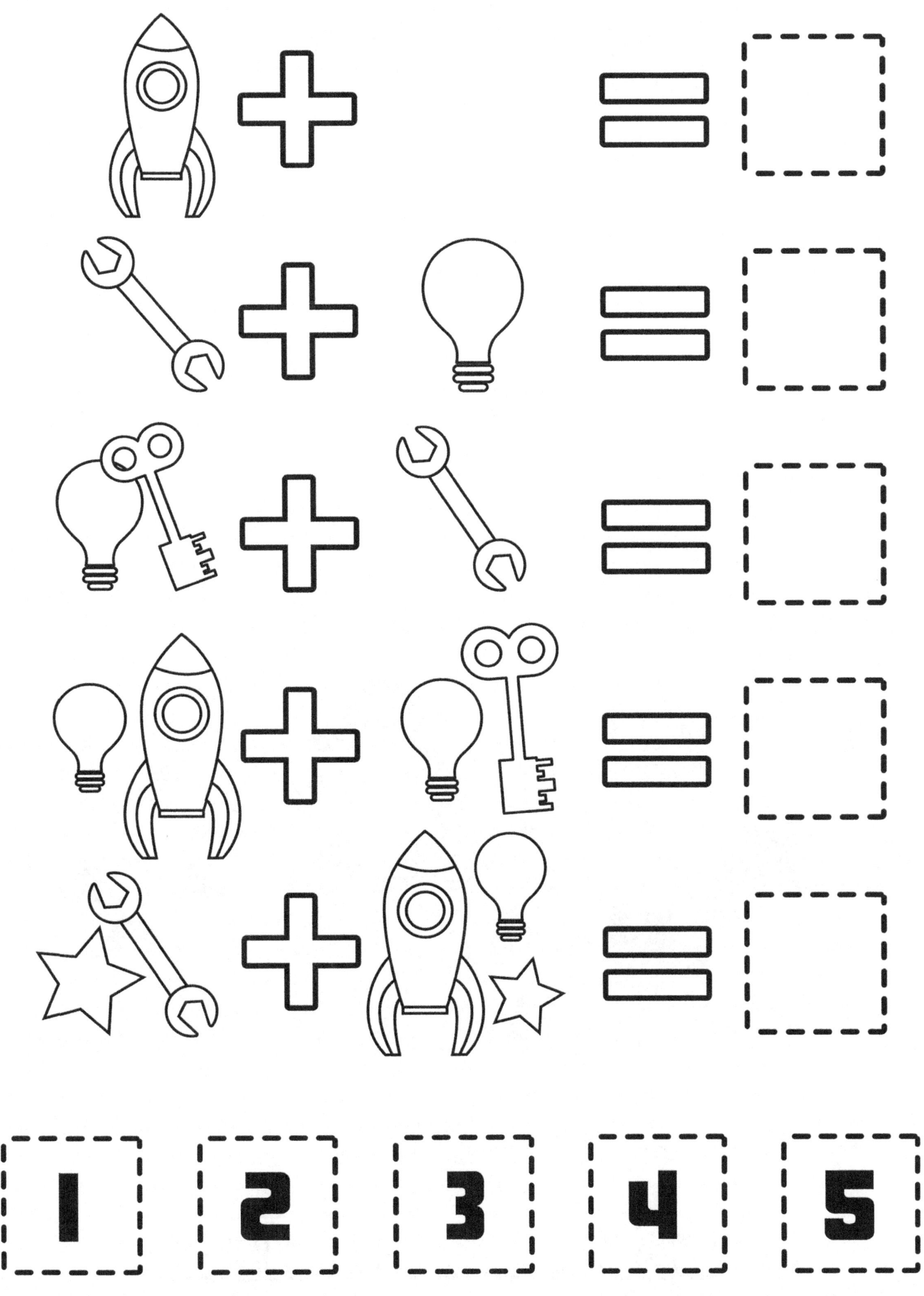

HOW MANY PIRATES DO YOU SEE?

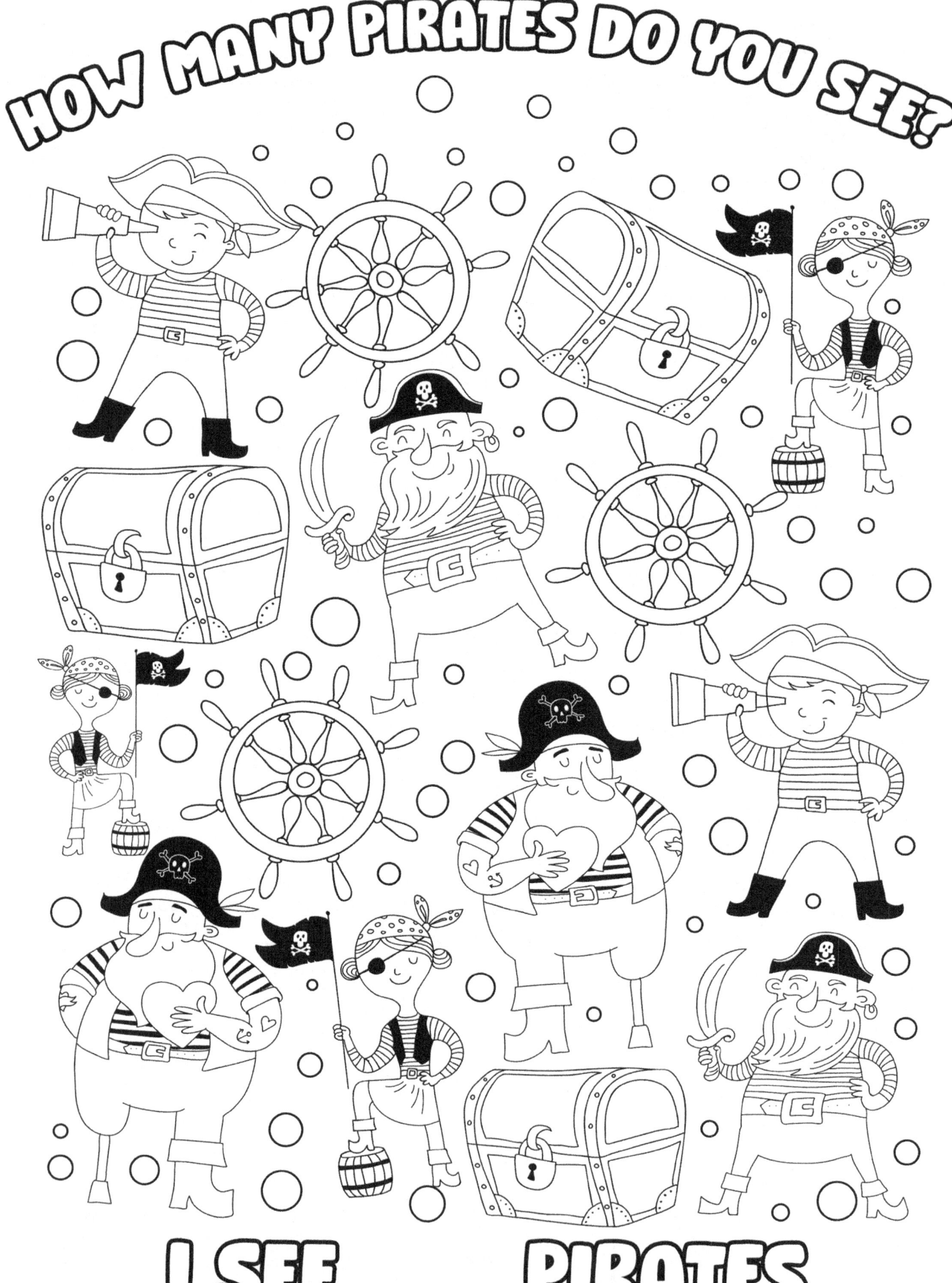

I SEE _____ PIRATES

COMPLETE THE PICTURE

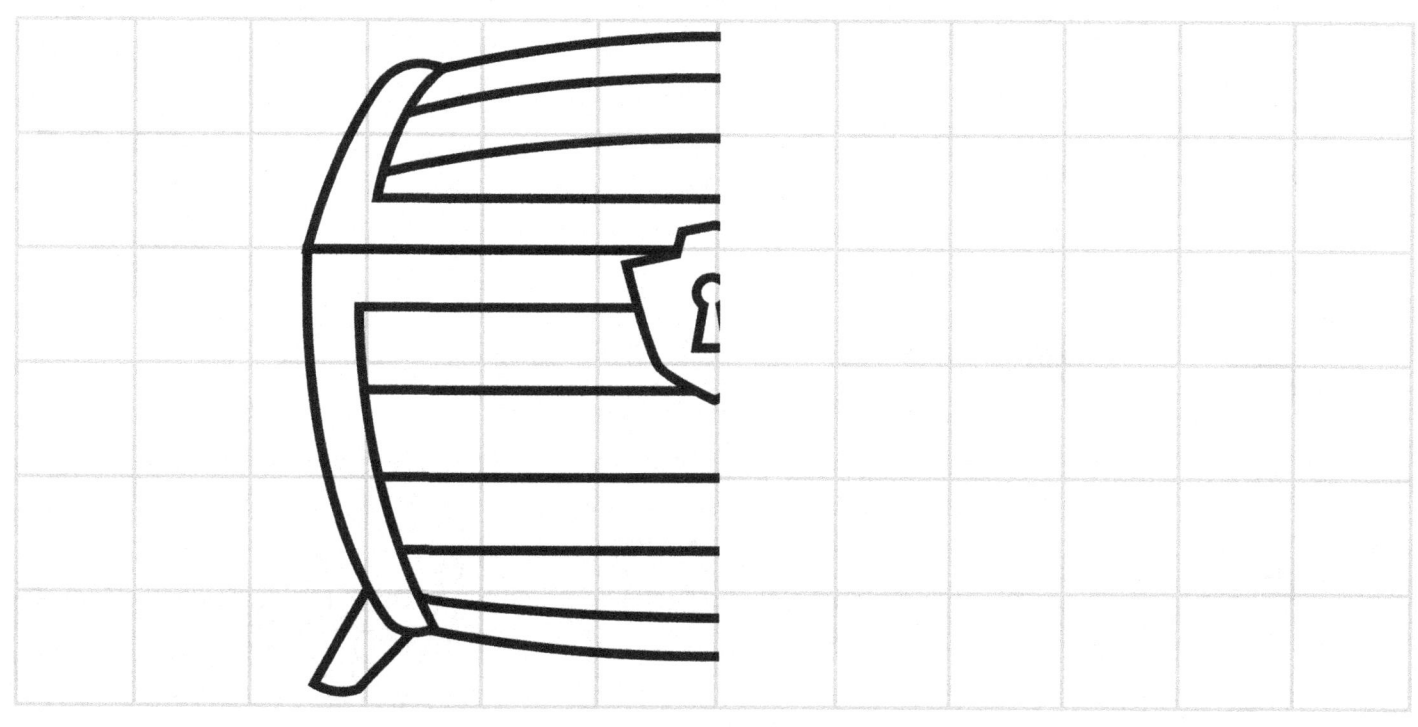

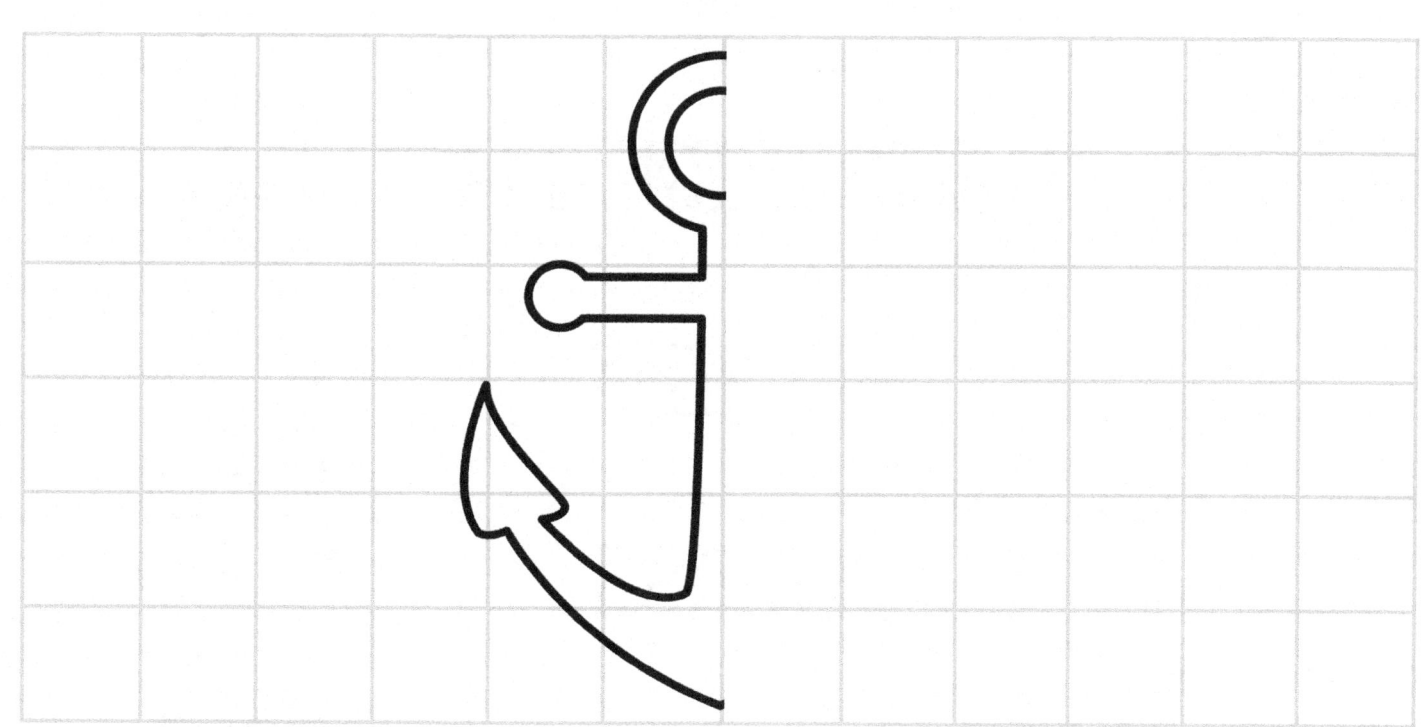

MATCH WORD TO PICTURE

CLOUD

PALM

LIGHTHOUSE

CHEST

BARREL

SMOKING PIPE

PIRATE

SHARK

FIND THE TEN DIFFERENCES BETWEEN THE TWO PICTURES

COUNT AND COLOR

FIND ②MATCHING ITEMS

P	A	C	P	Y	B	D	F	P
L	A	N	A	S	K	U	L	L
C	N	Z	R	M	M	S	A	N
R	C	I	R	A	X	K	G	E
N	H	C	O	P	C	U	X	Q
A	O	E	T	V	D	J	L	I
W	R	P	I	R	A	T	E	W
F	I	S	H	D	V	L	Q	A
P	U	G	F	S	H	I	P	T

COPY THE PICTURE

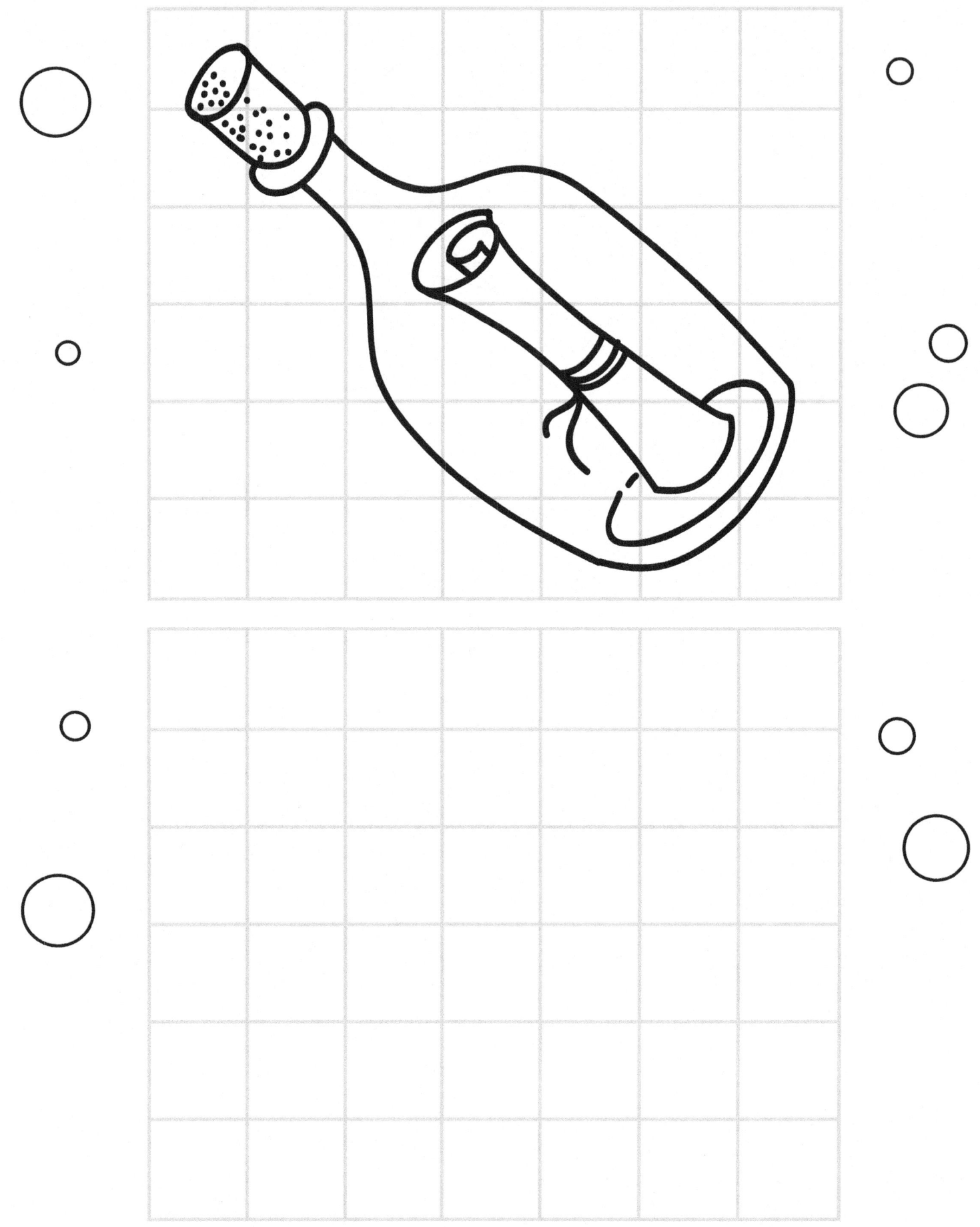

COMPLETE THE PICTURE

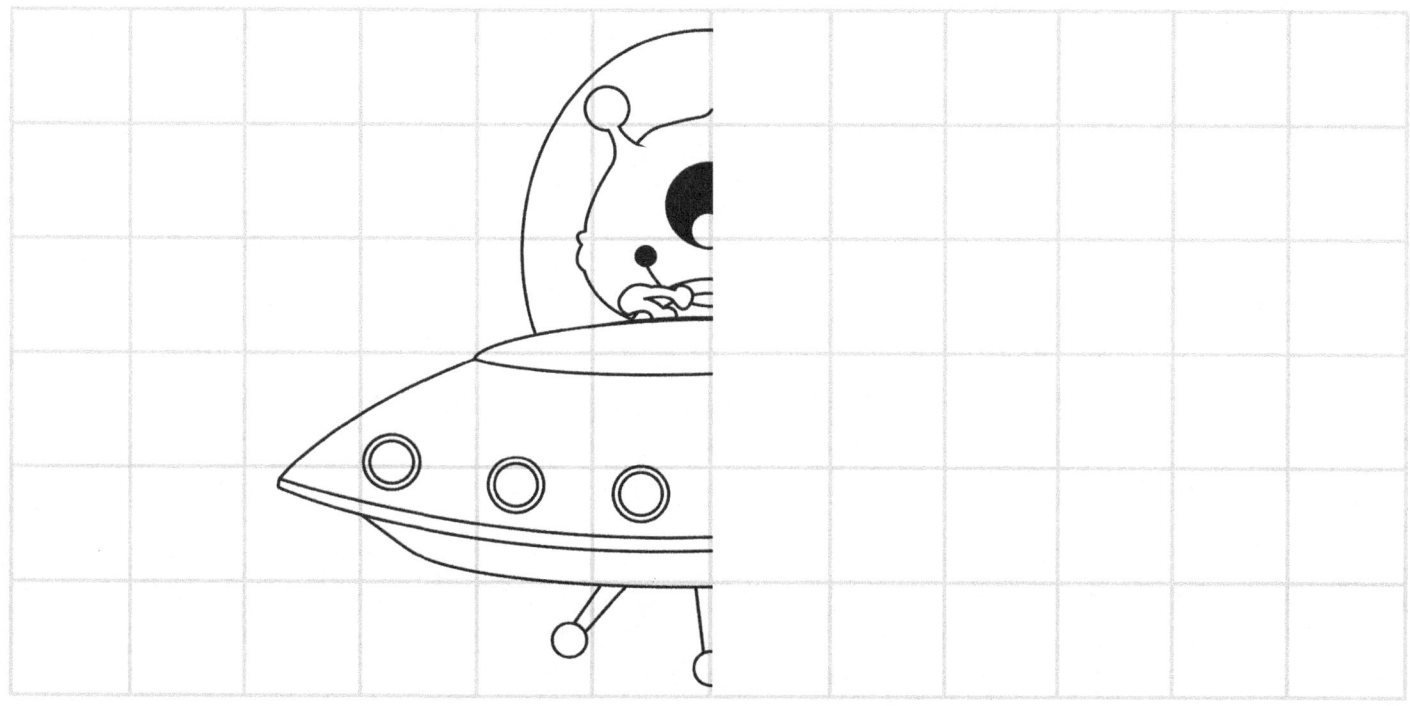

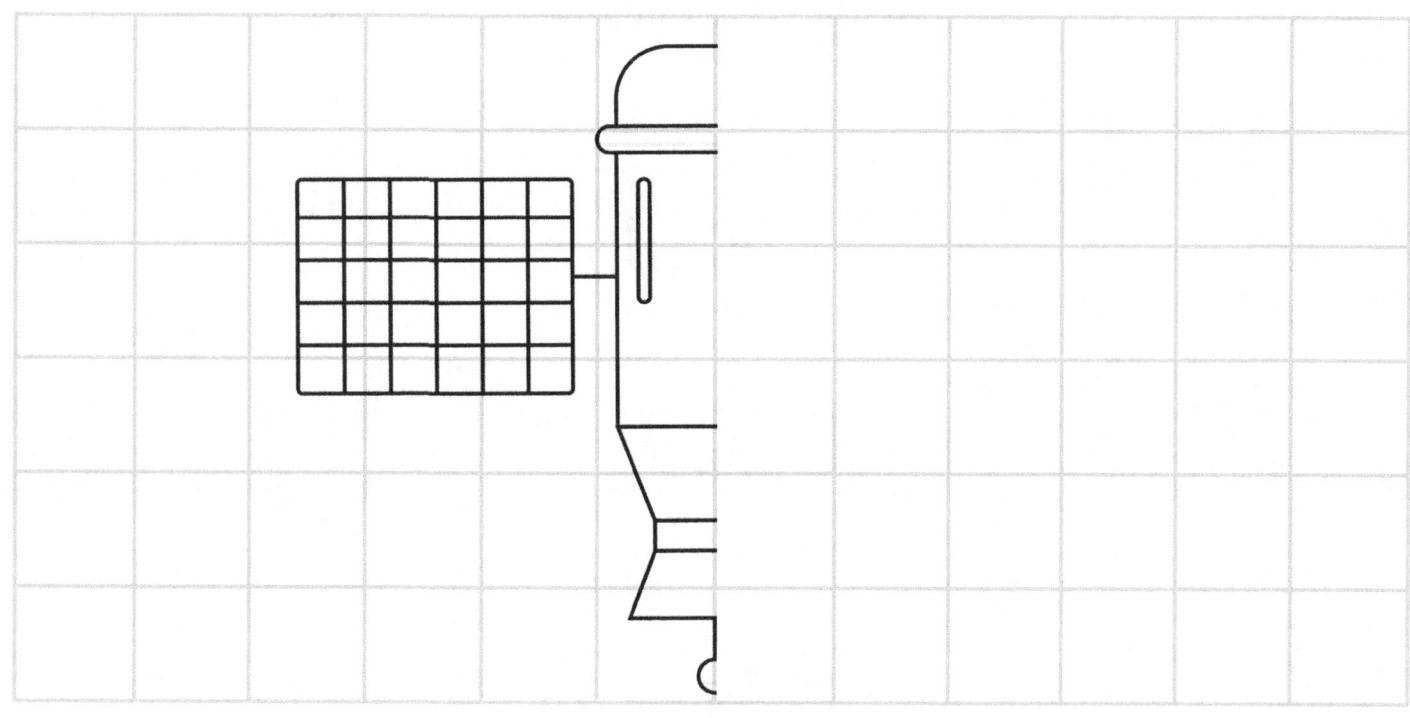

MATCH WORD TO PICTURE

ROCKET

FLAG

SATURN

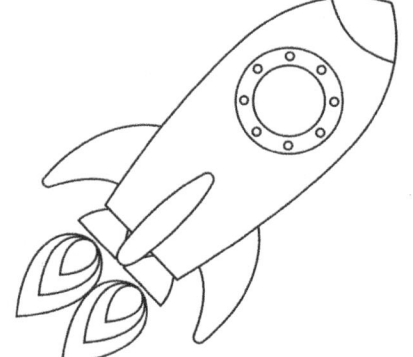

SATELLITE

TELESCOPE

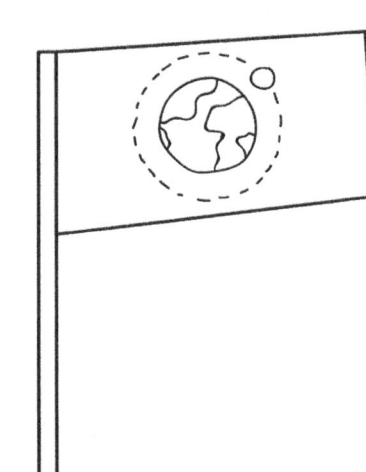

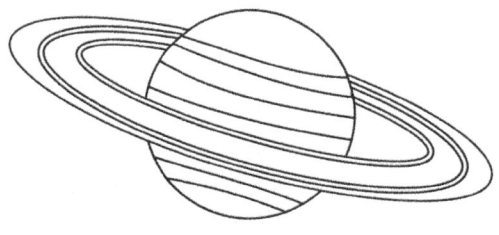

ALIEN

COMET

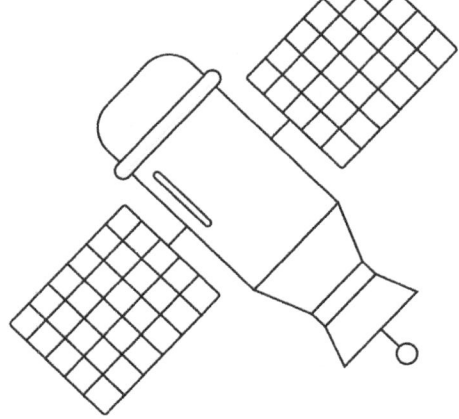

STAR

FIND THE TEN DIFFERENCES BETWEEN THE TWO PICTURES

COUNT AND COLOR

FIND ② MATCHING ITEMS

```
A S T E R O I D
C J U P I T E R
P S U N B A K U
R O C K E T Y K
Q P E I F L A G
R A Z J B X A G
B P H C X W J O
C O M E T R Y F
```

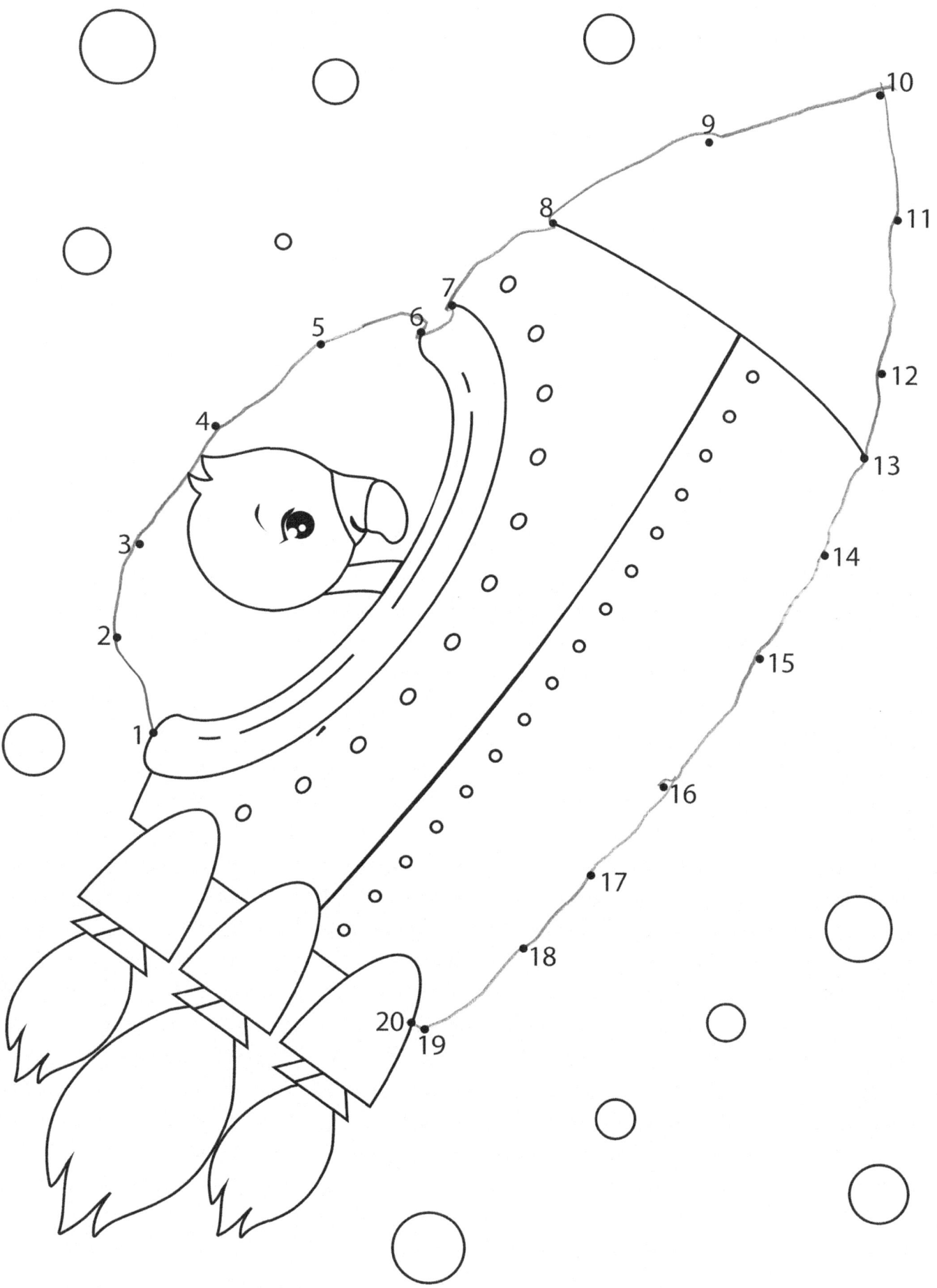

COPY THE PICTURE

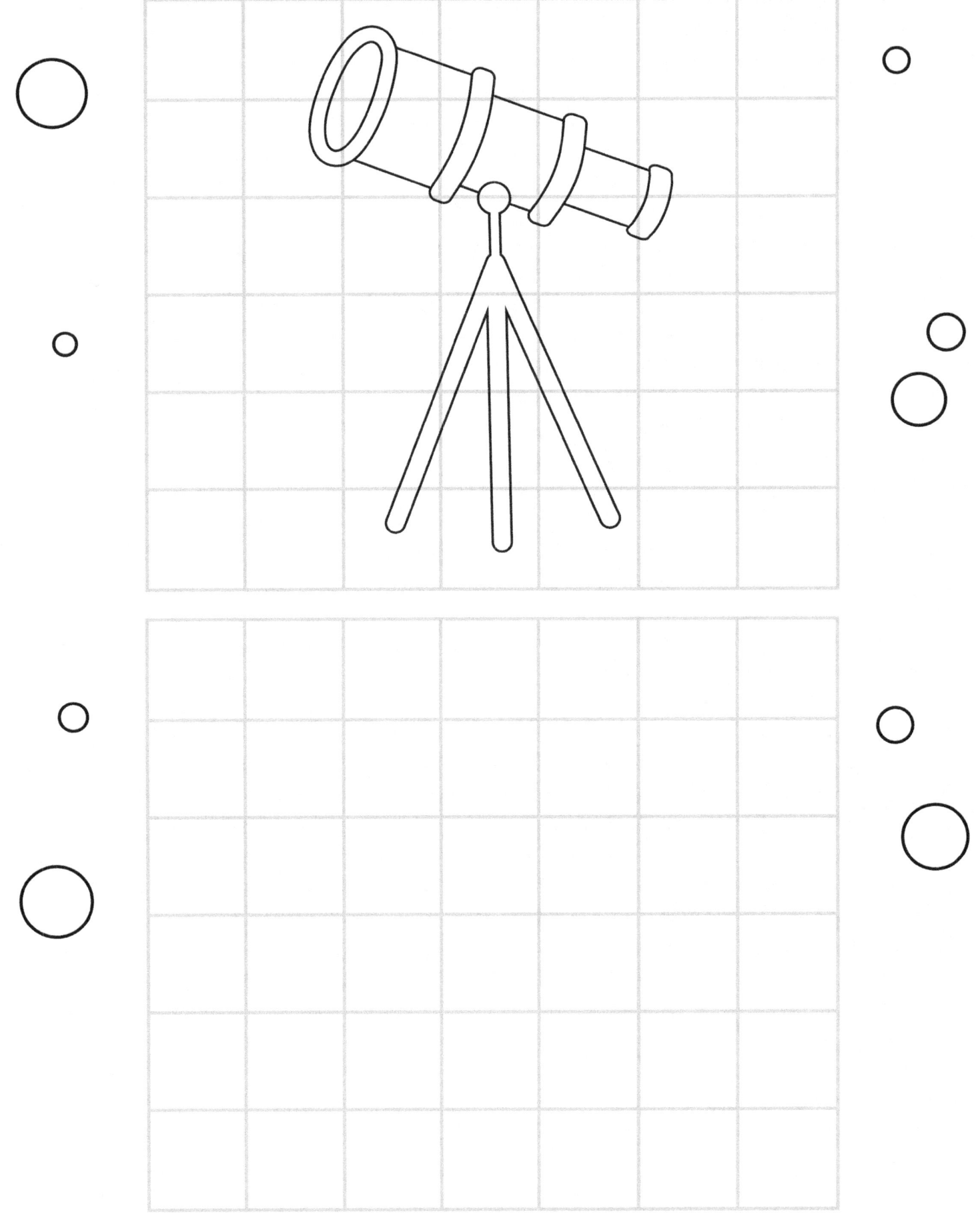

HOW MANY SHELLS DO YOU SEE?

I SEE _____ SHELLS

COMPLETE THE PICTURE

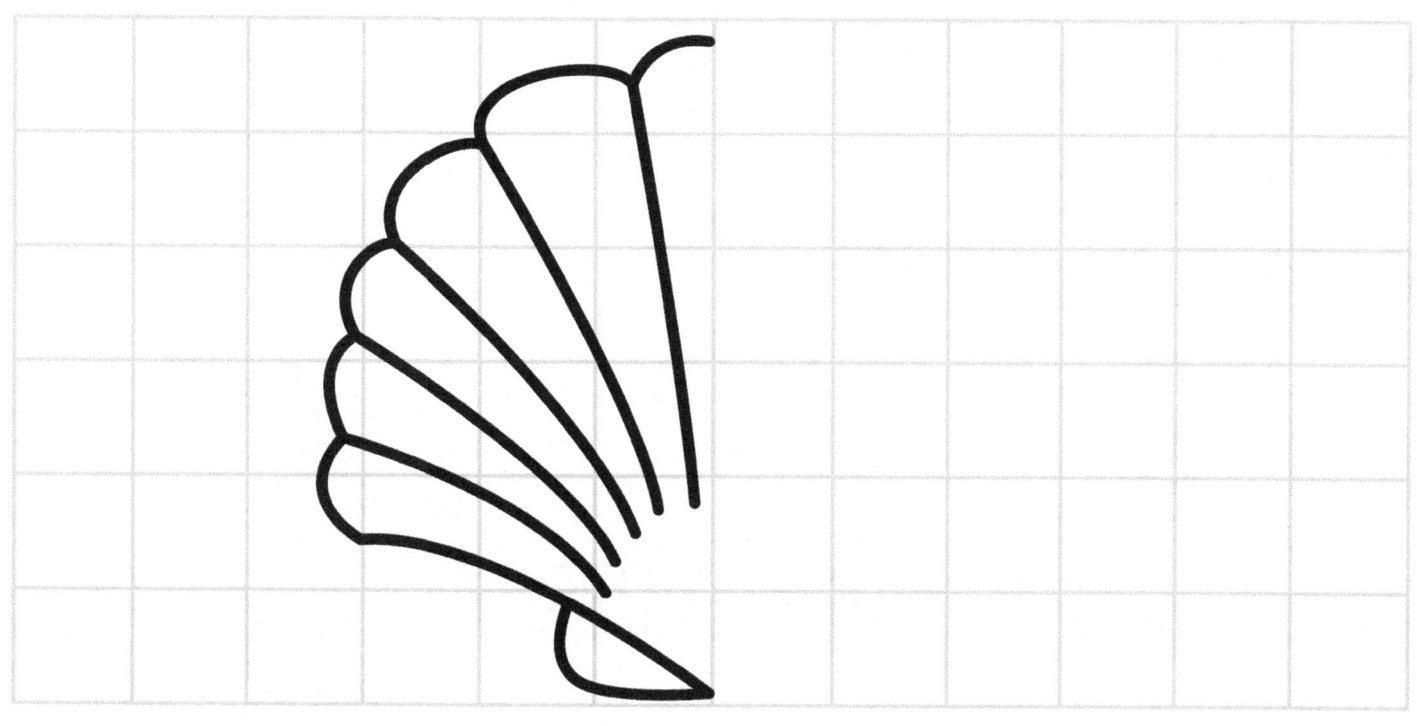

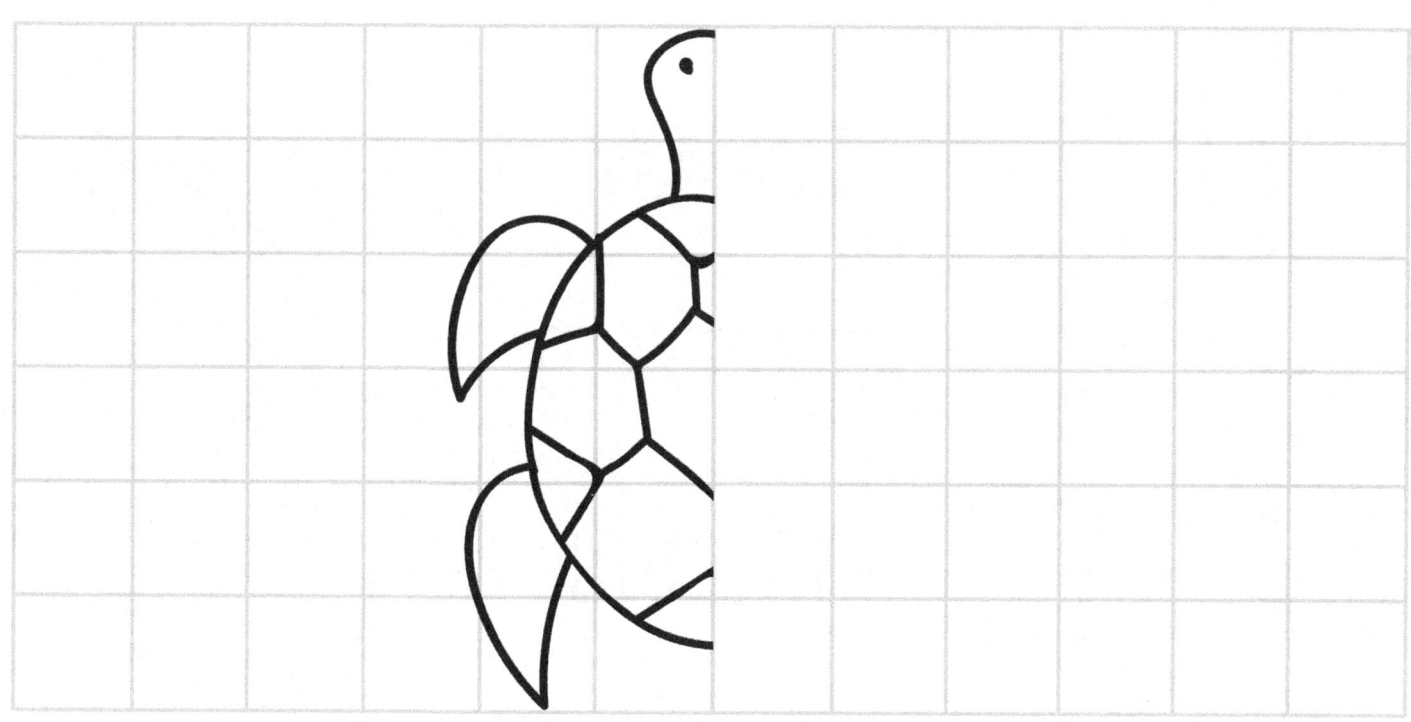

MATCH WORD TO PICTURE

MERMAID

SHELL

CRAB

OCTOPUS

SEA HORSE

TURTLE

JELLYFISH

ANCHOR

FIND THE TEN DIFFERENCES BETWEEN THE TWO PICTURES

COUNT AND COLOR

FIND ② MATCHING ITEMS

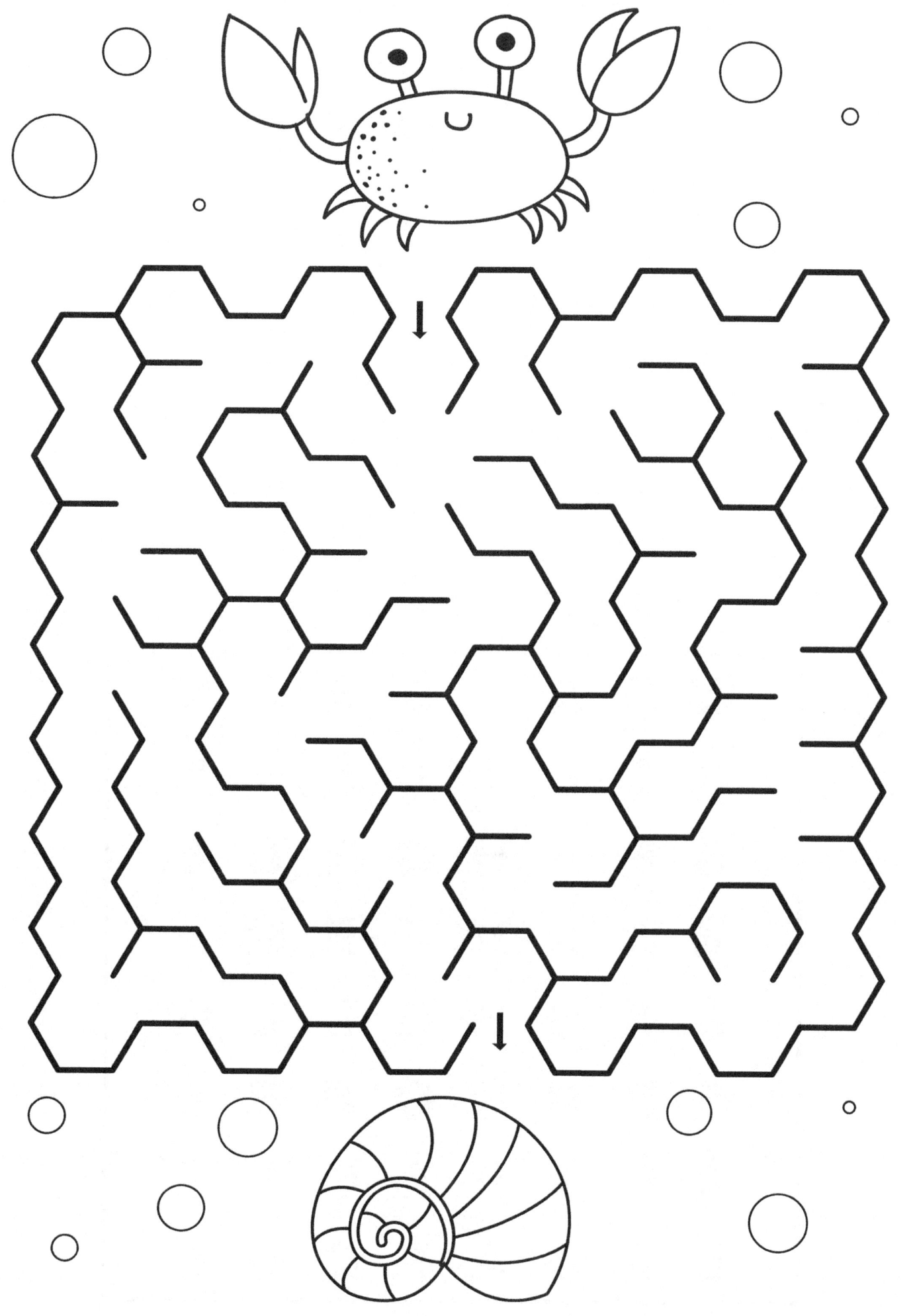

```
W H A L E A Z V
D E L I L S J S
S E A H O R S E
M W A V E E M A
F X S H E L L W
E P P Q O H B E
R M I R R O R E
L R O A F Q S D
```

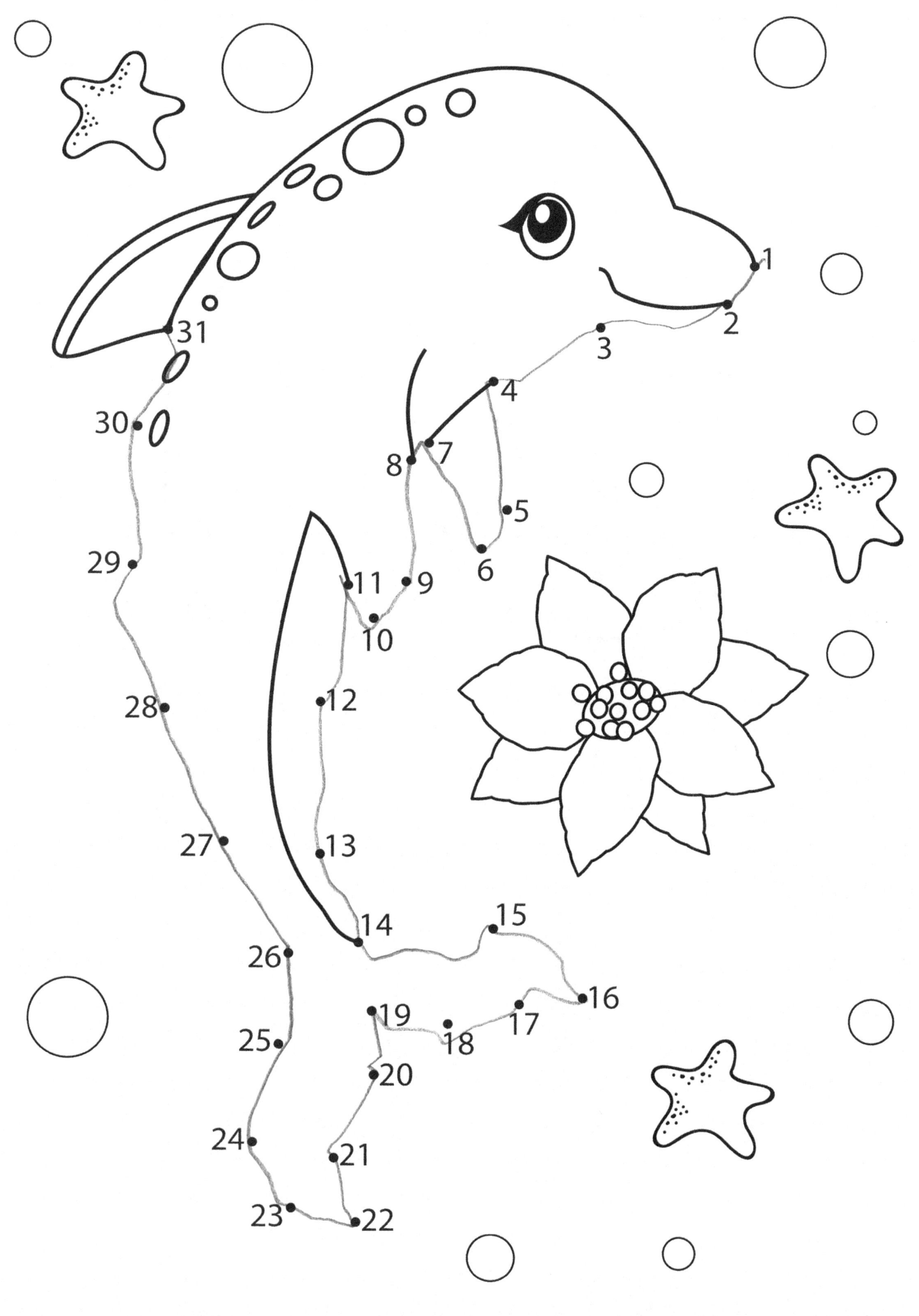

COPY THE PICTURE

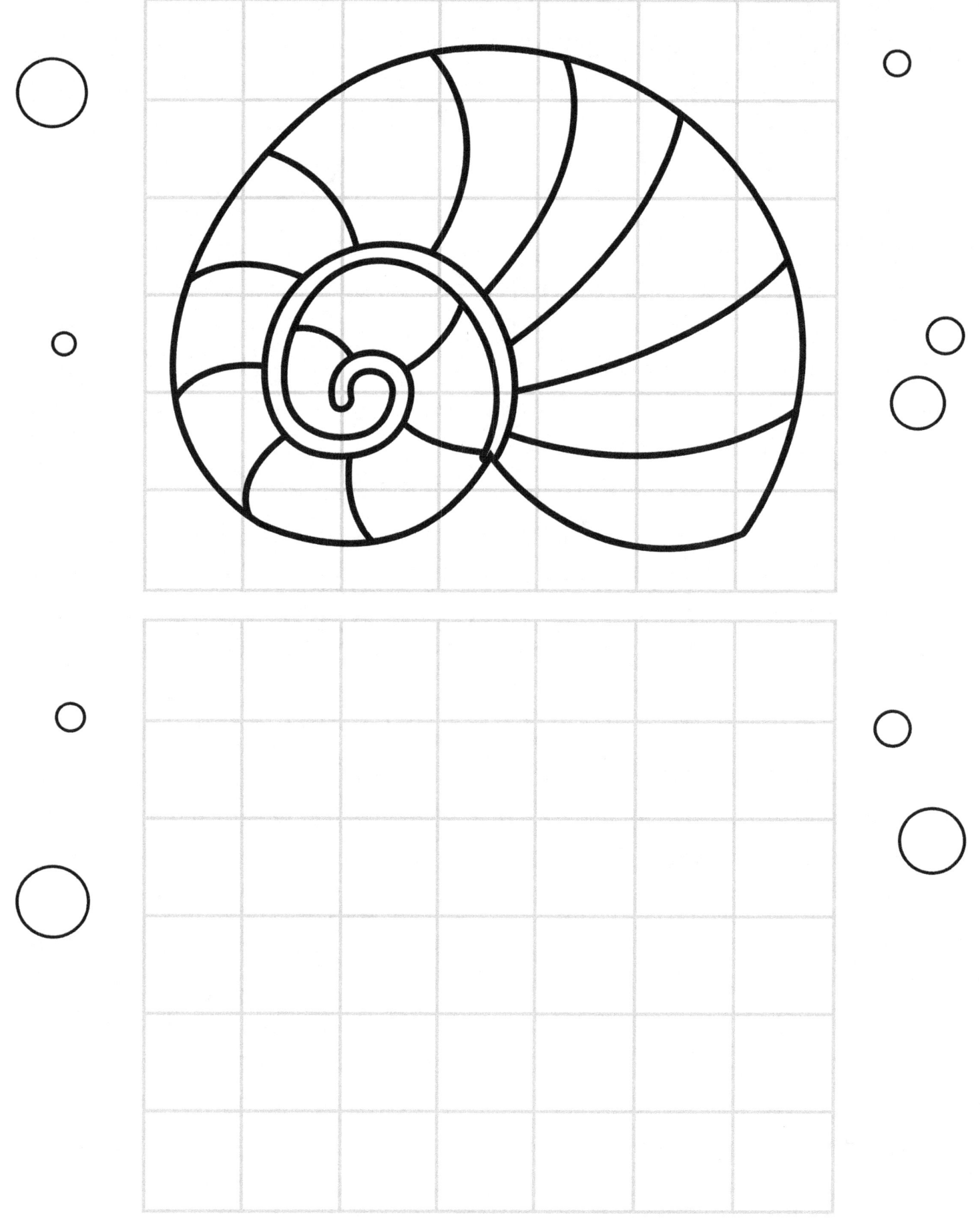

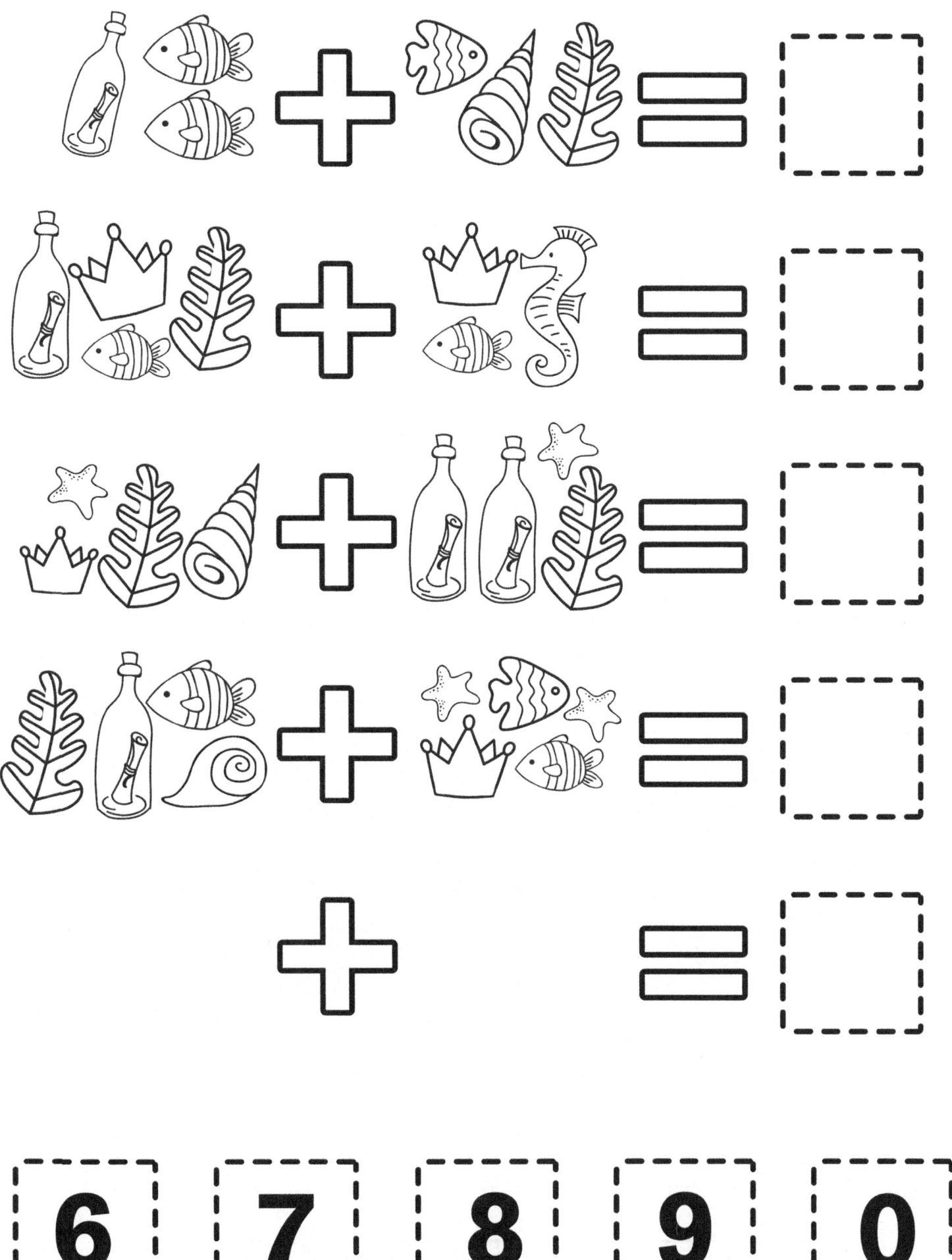

COMPLETE THE PICTURE

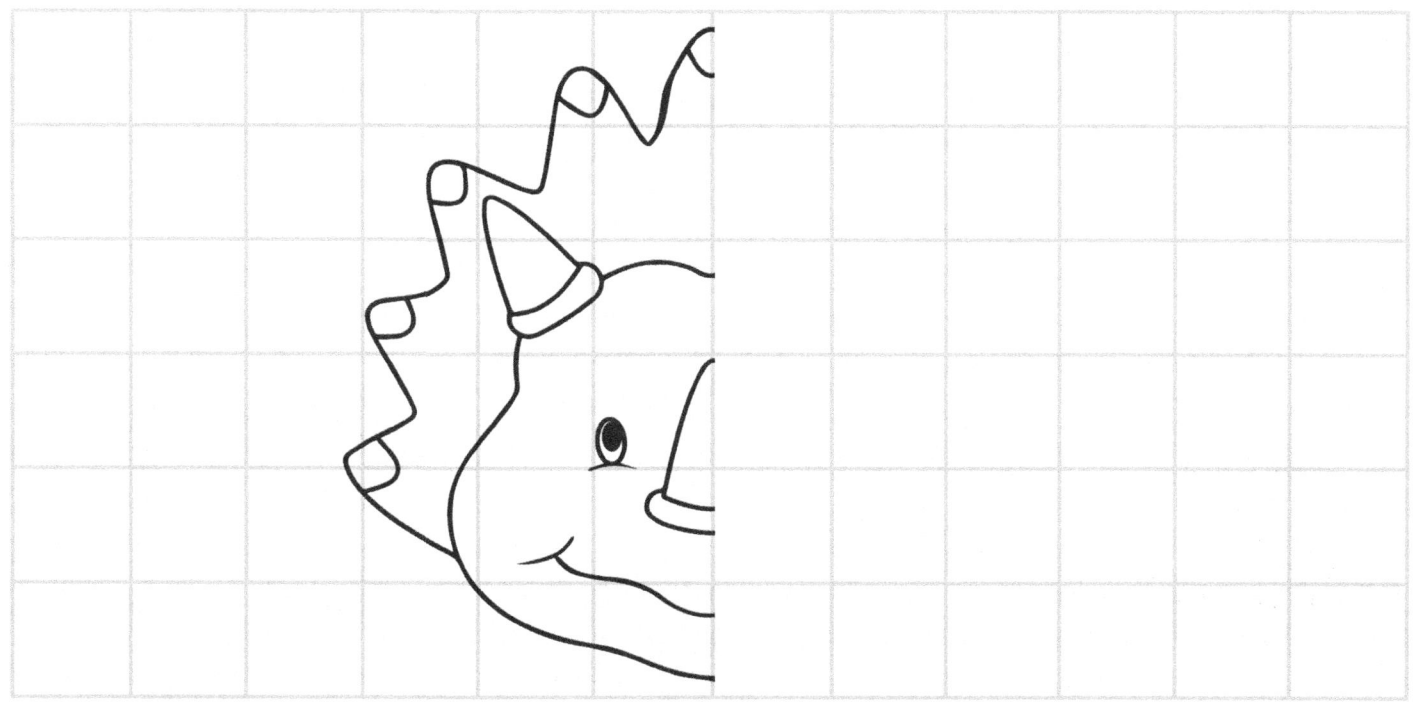

MATCH WORD TO PICTURE

LEAF

FLOWER

T-REX

NEST

ISLAND

SKULL

DINOSAUR

VOLCANO

FIND THE TEN DIFFERENCES BETWEEN THE TWO PICTURES

COUNT AND COLOR

FIND ② MATCHING ITEMS

S	F	O	E	G	G	D	K
A	P	A	L	M	W	O	Z
D	I	N	O	S	A	U	R
B	E	F	L	O	W	E	R
Y	H	R	L	Y	R	T	X
M	E	B	E	L	J	R	X
N	J	O	A	N	Y	E	Y
X	A	J	F	B	V	X	A

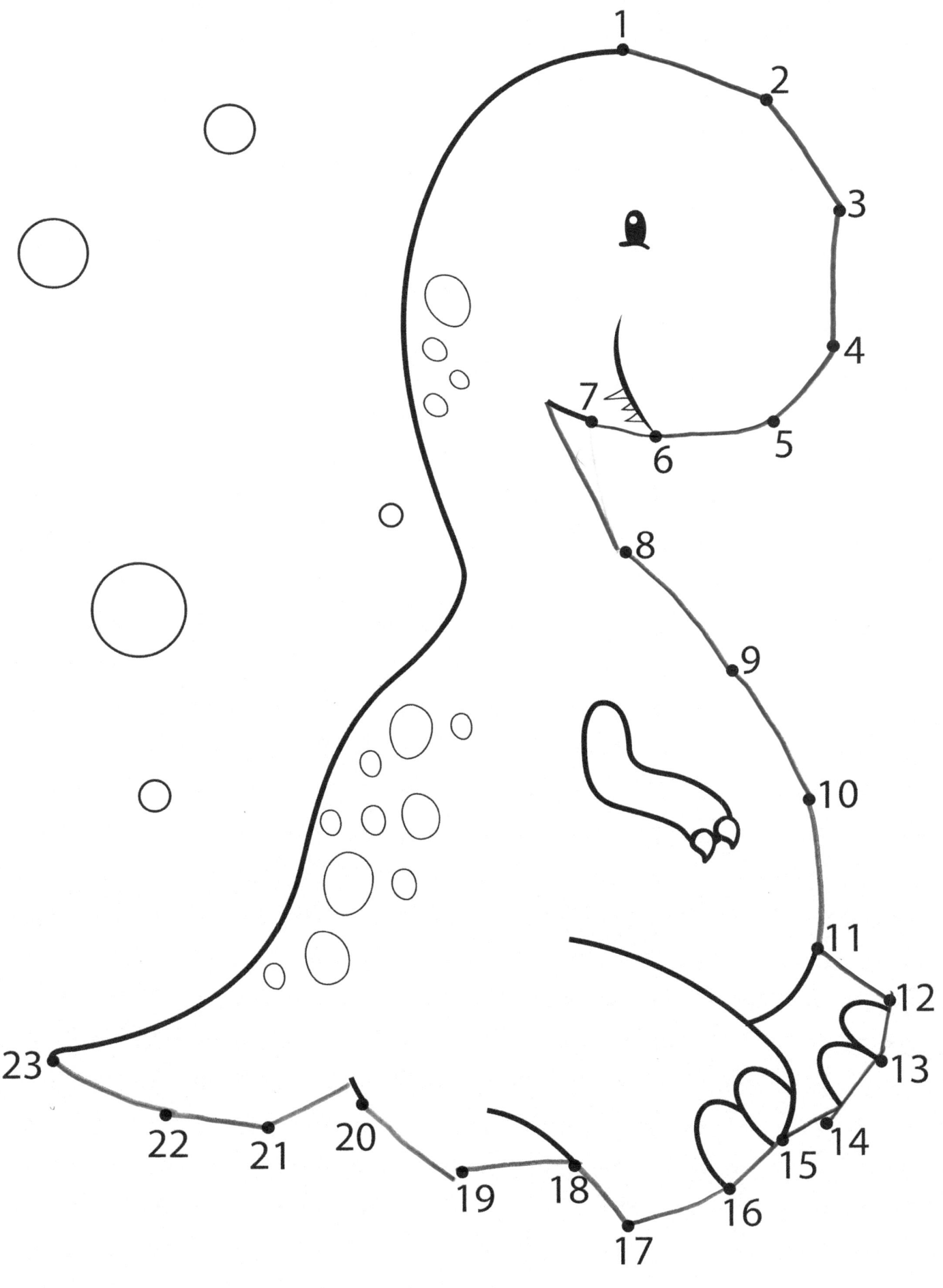

COPY THE PICTURE

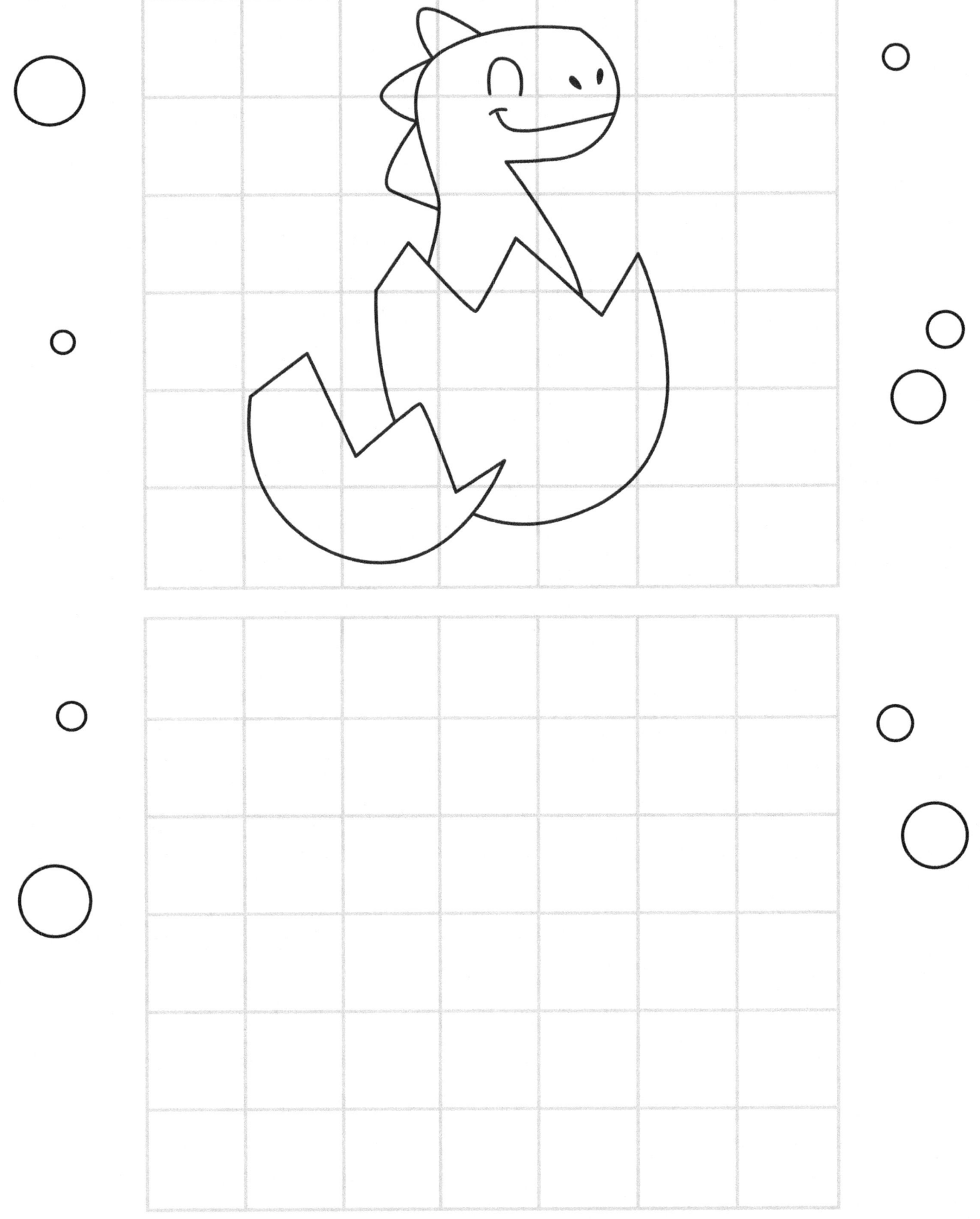

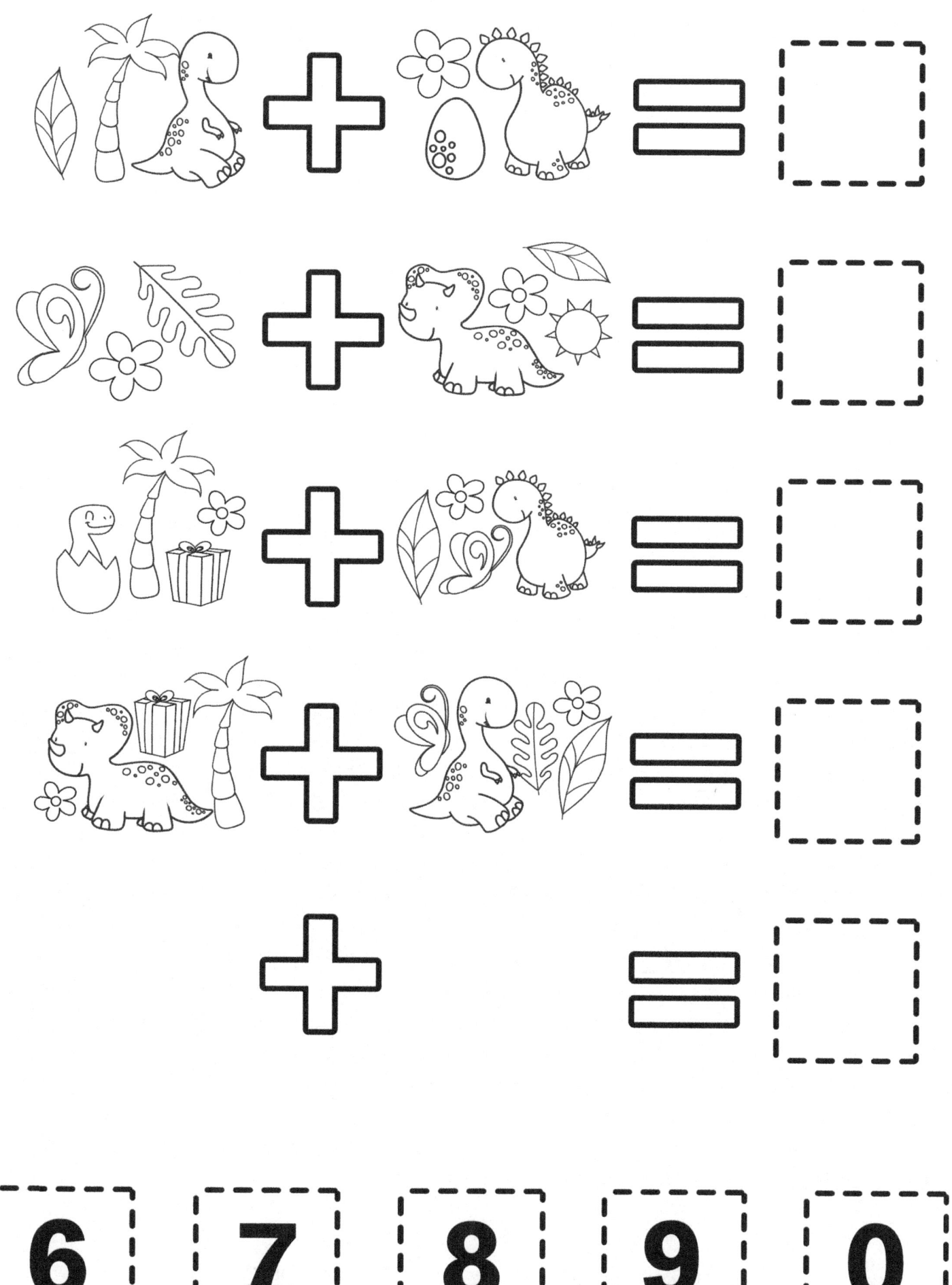

HOW MANY TREES DO YOU SEE?

I SEE ____ TREES

COMPLETE THE PICTURE

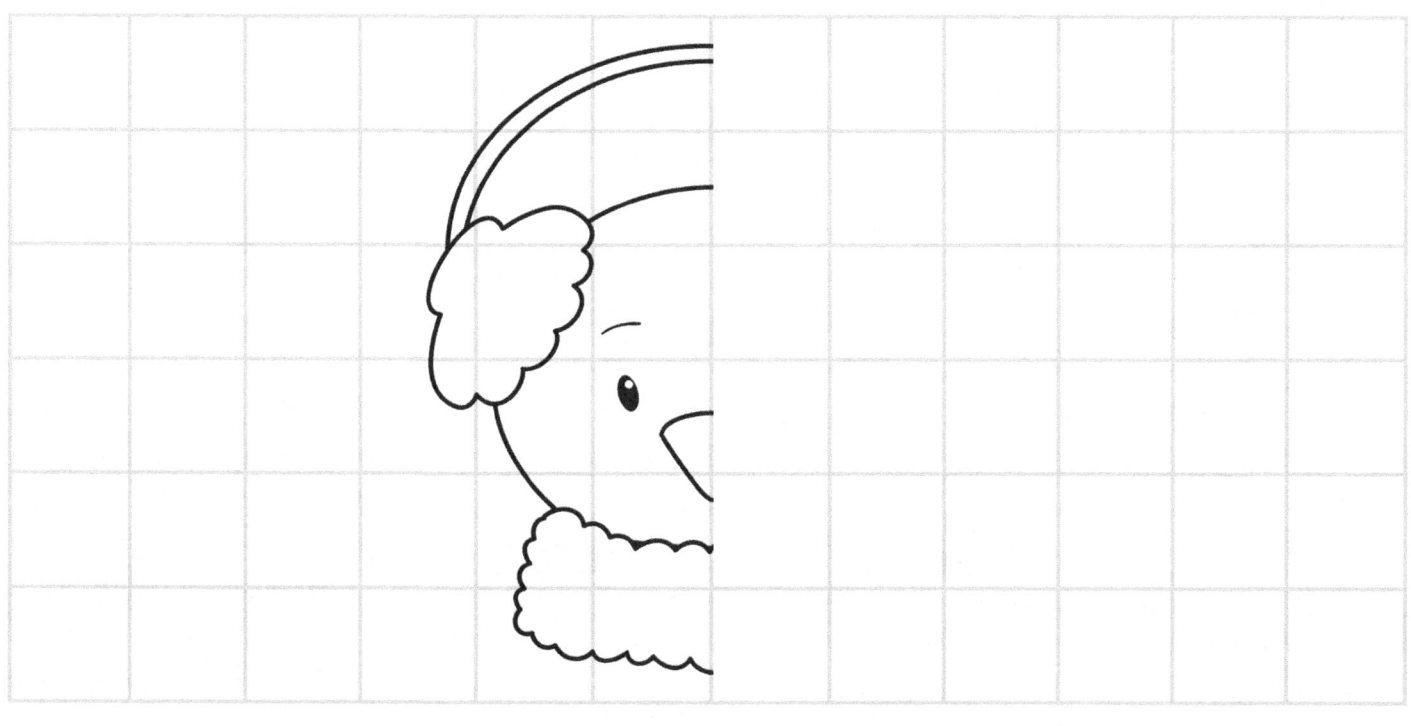

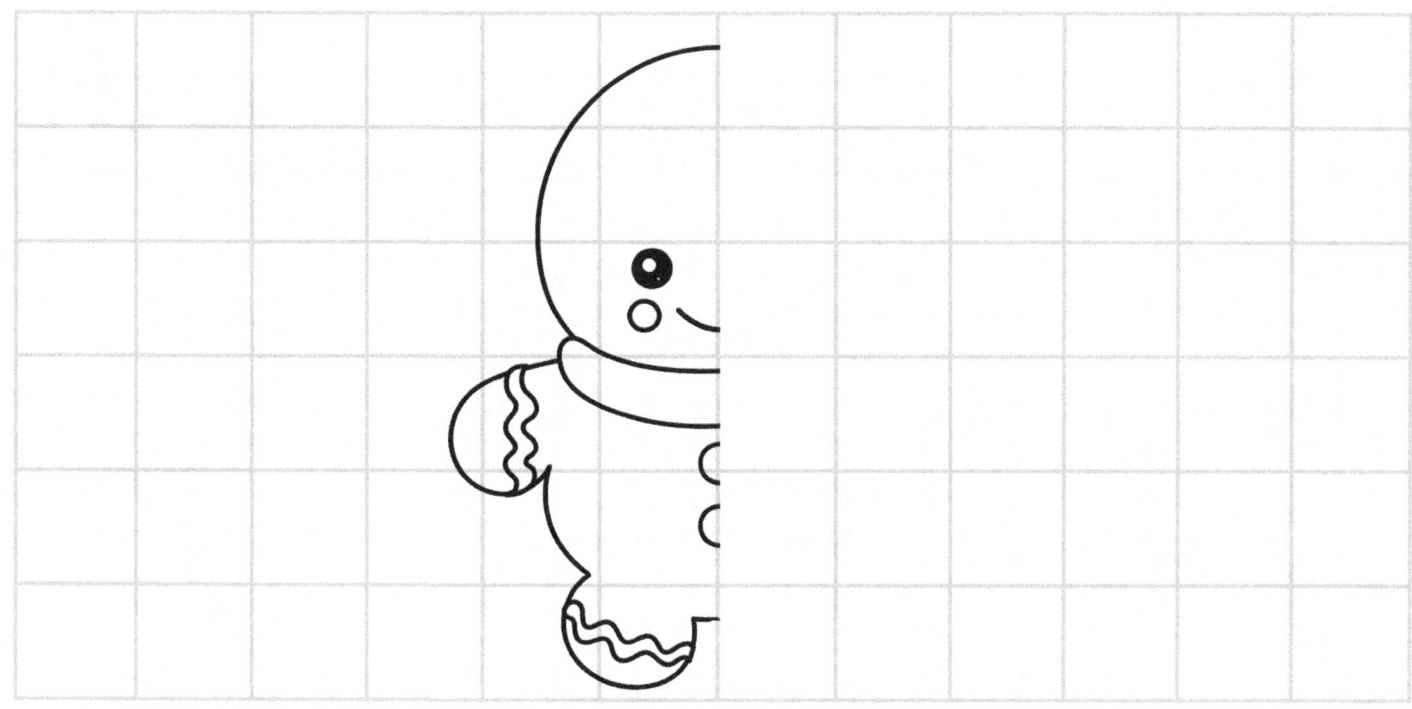

MATCH WORD TO PICTURE

CACTUS

OWL

WREATH

GINGERBREAD

CHICKEN

STAR

UNICORN

SANTA

HOUSE

FIND THE TEN DIFFERENCES BETWEEN THE TWO PICTURES

COUNT AND COLOR

FIND 2 MATCHING ITEMS

```
P  V  C  S  T  A  R
G  I  F  T  W  Q  Z
C  E  L  D  R  S  T
A  S  O  C  E  A  R
N  E  A  C  A  N  E
D  N  D  J  T  T  E
Y  T  U  E  H  A  C
```

COPY THE PICTURE

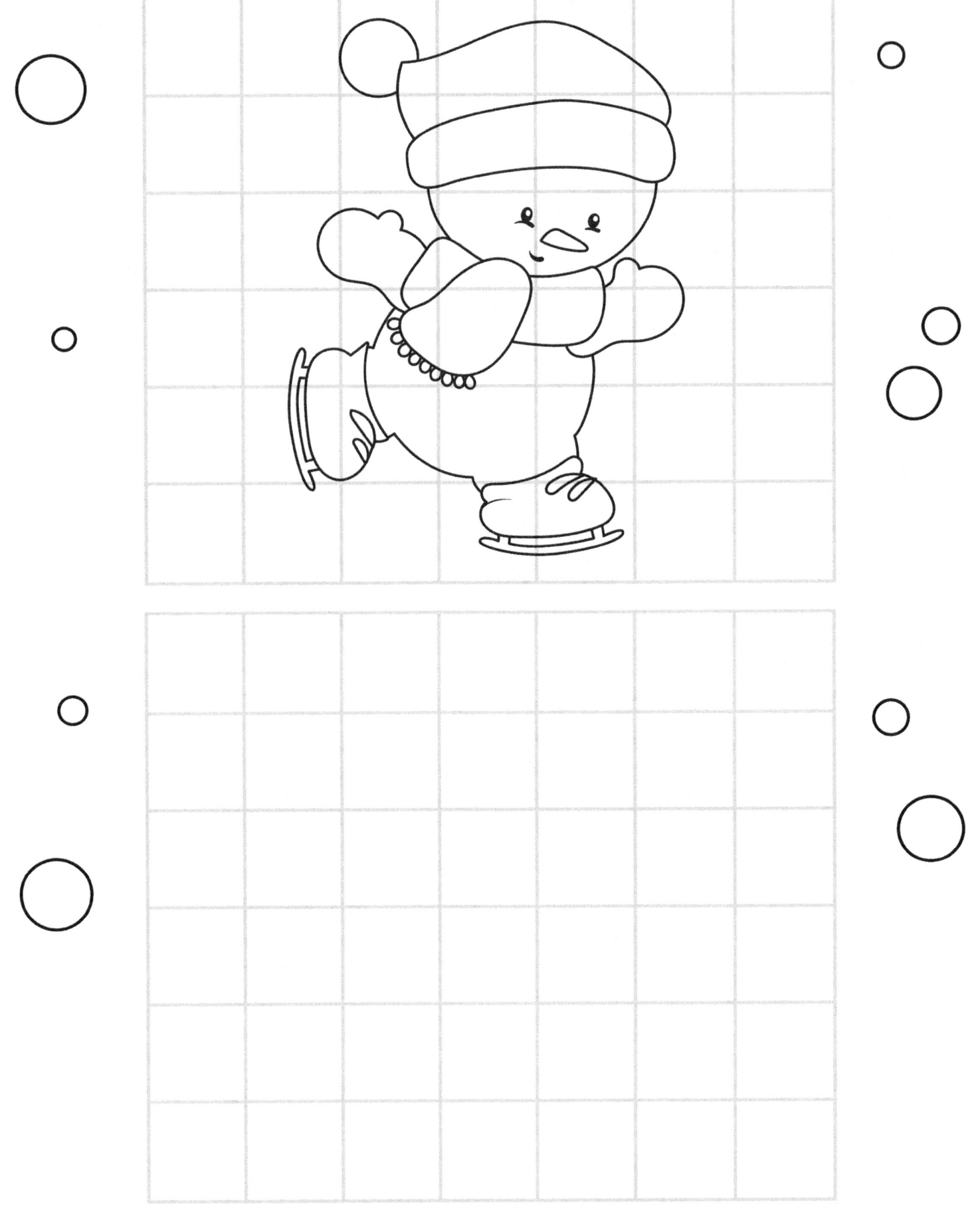

HOW MANY OWLS DO YOU SEE?

I SEE ____ OWLS

COMPLETE THE PICTURE

MATCH WORD TO PICTURE

COW

HORSE

CHICKEN

DOG

SHEEP

PIGGY

DEER

DOLPHIN

FIND THE TEN DIFFERENCES BETWEEN THE TWO PICTURES

COUNT AND COLOR

FIND 2 MATCHING ITEMS

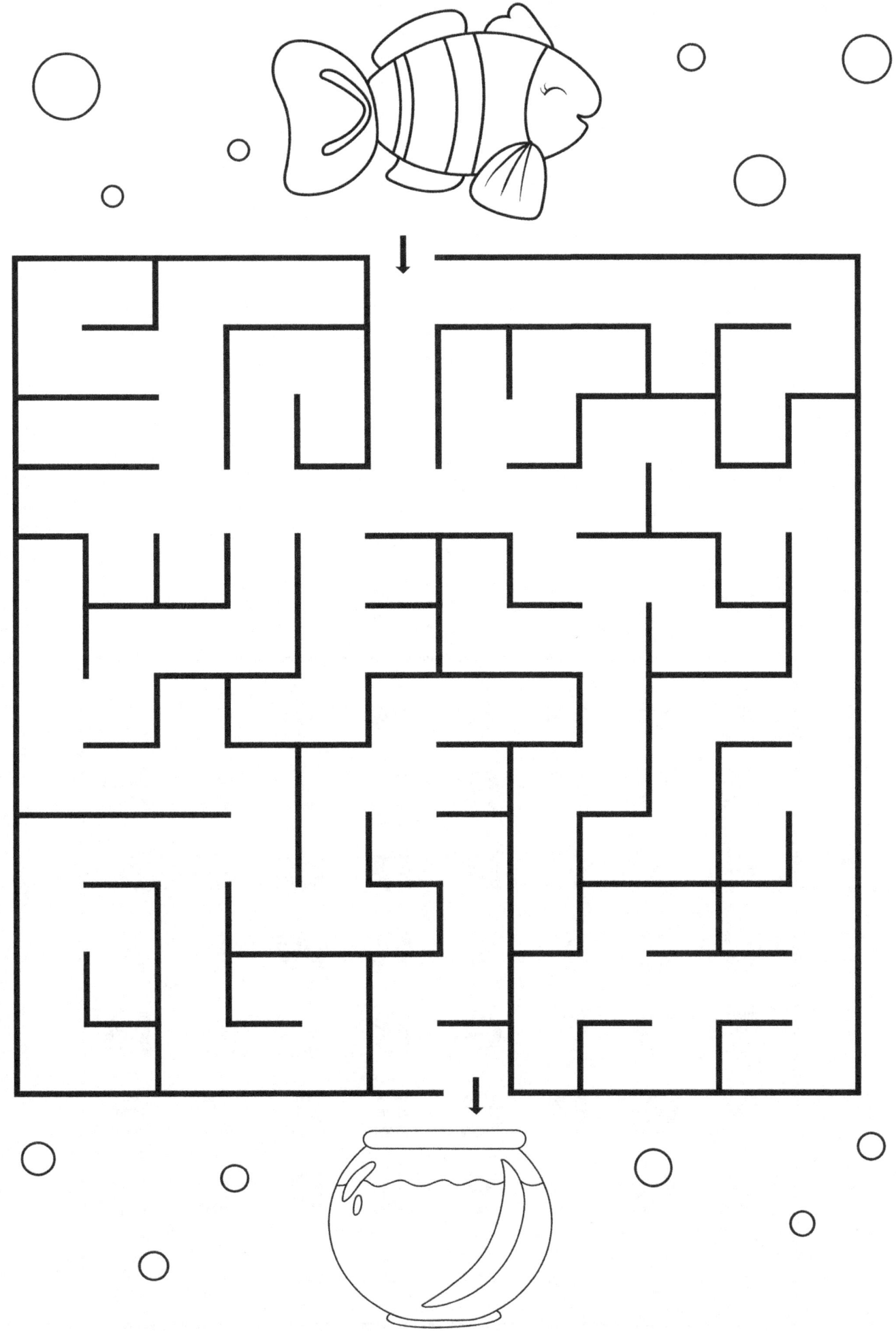

I	E	W	L	A	V	F	I
X	U	O	R	D	J	L	M
F	X	C	P	D	O	G	X
G	C	T	I	B	W	E	Z
E	O	O	G	B	L	K	M
N	W	P	G	E	A	X	E
Z	Q	U	Y	A	G	L	B
F	Y	S	I	R	M	L	X

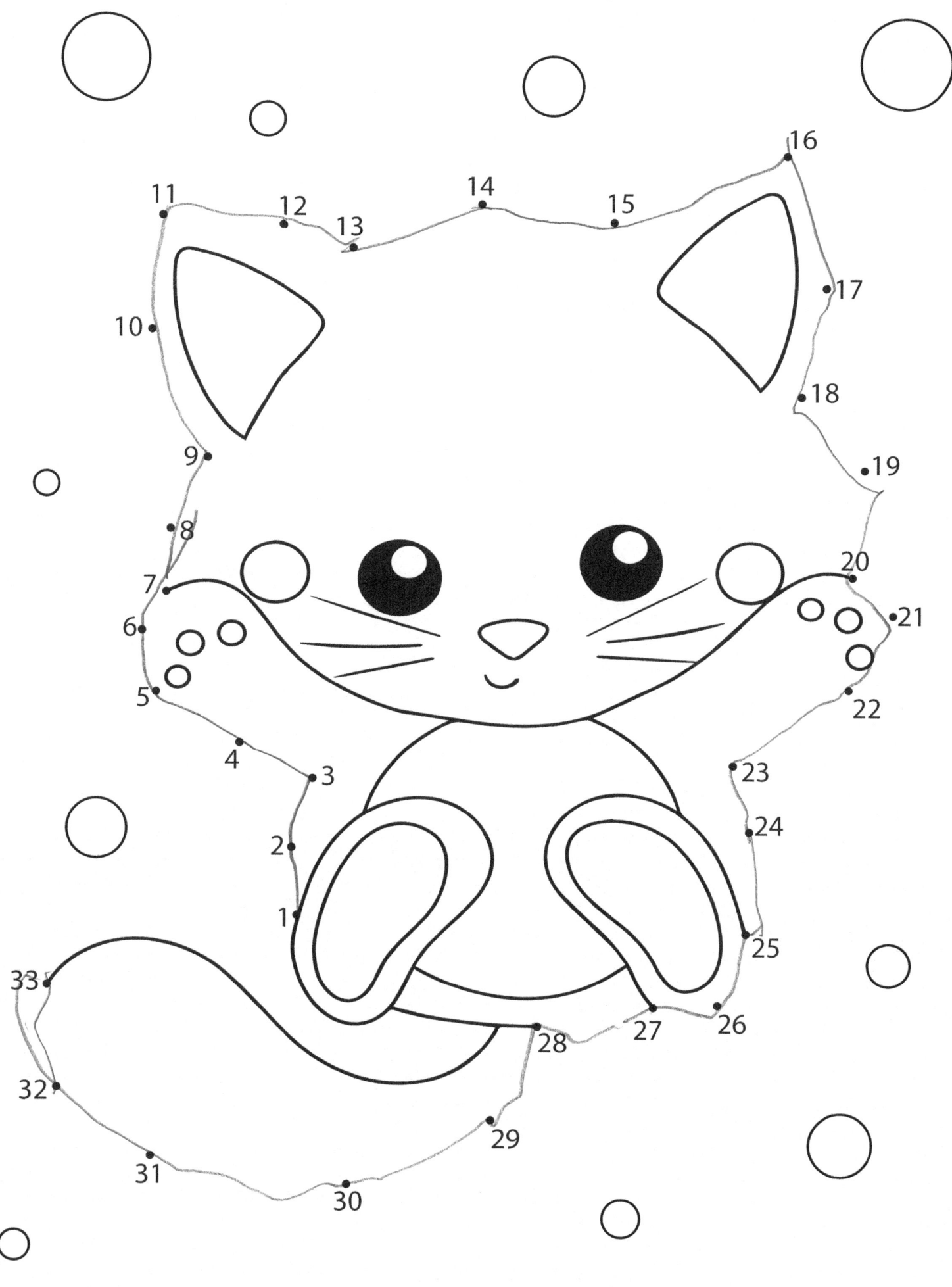

COPY THE PICTURE

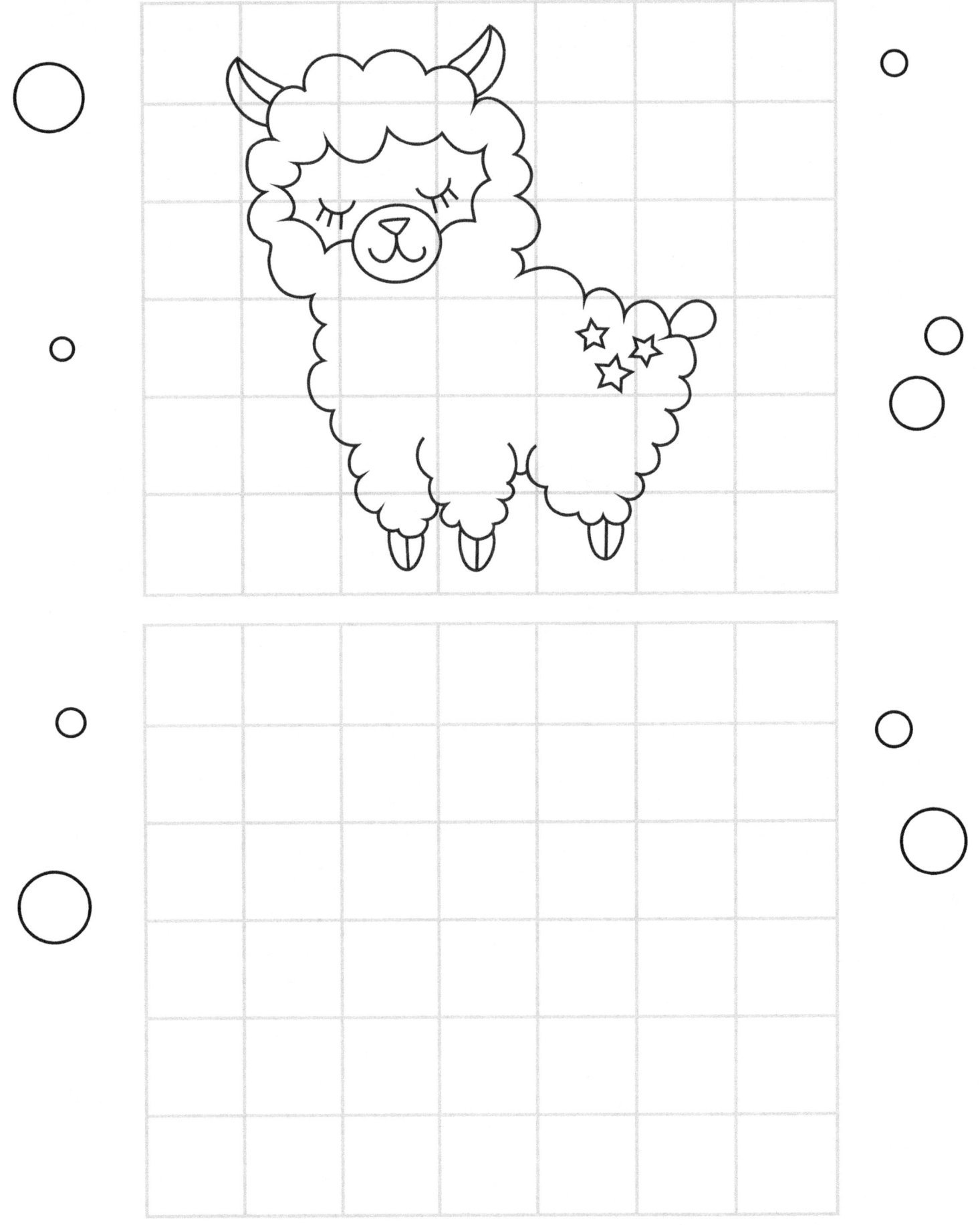

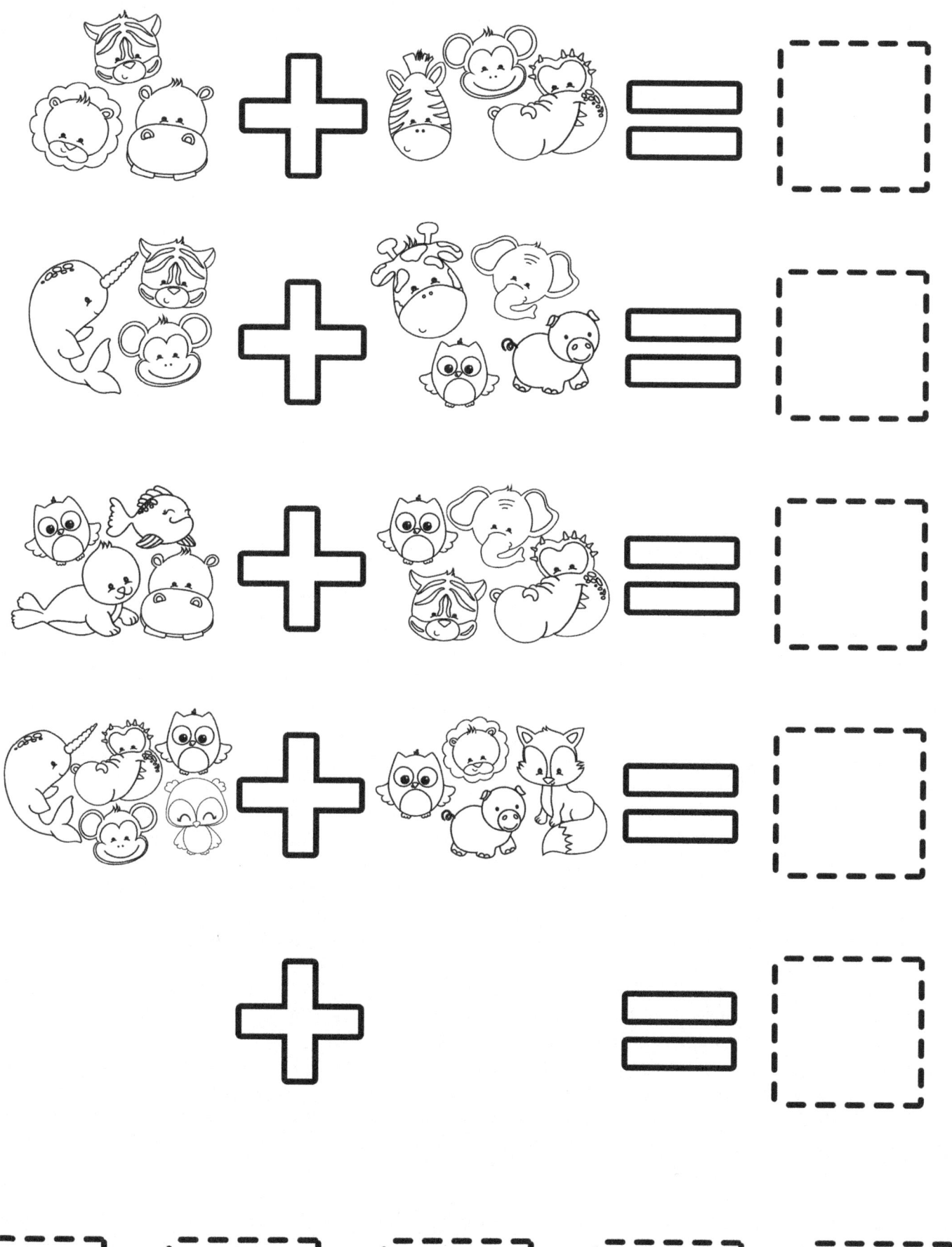

Made in the USA
Coppell, TX
10 December 2022